Praise for *The Unexpected Leader*

The Unexpected Leader is a quite remarkable book full of subtle and important insights. Using the professional and personal life stories of a range of leaders, Iesha shines a light on the varied routes into leadership roles. The beautifully crafted accounts of individual stories combined with her own experiences create a rich hinterland to the motivations, the fears and the joys of this work. It is an important read for all in education and will be particularly helpful for young leaders who might be doubting themselves. Heart-warming, inspiring and insightful in equal measure.

Mary Myatt, writer and school improvement adviser

Honest, open, insightful and, above all, fascinating. Iesha Small has written a seriously important book about educational leadership.

Jeffrey Boakye, teacher and author of *Hold Tight: Black Masculinity, Millennials and the Meaning of Grime*

Iesha Small's quiet strength shines through this book via the conversations she has with others who may not fit the more commonly held preconceptions of what people who run schools are actually like. Providing a fascinatingly human insight into what it takes to manage (in more ways than one) in an educational setting, Iesha talks to those who have followed their own paths to positions of leadership and also offers her own unique story as a way of broadening the narrative around the people who take on this great responsibility.

Tom Starkey, education consultant and writer

What teachers need now is a frank and open discussion on the ways in which teaching can impact upon them as individuals, and *The Unexpected Leader* is full to the brim with the sheer humanity of the profession – with the highs and the lows laid out for us all to share.

Authenticity has always been Iesha Small's watchword – it doesn't get much more authentic than this book. A must-read.

Bennie Kara, Deputy Head Teacher, Aureus School

While hundreds of titles have already been published on the demands and complexities of school leadership, this brave and honest book explores the issues of workload, imposter syndrome and mental health through the stories of real people. Between these accounts and Iesha's own personal insights, the implications of the challenges facing the education system – such as funding, accountability and teacher recruitment and retention – are all brought to life. Iesha's refreshingly simple yet convincing narrative challenges the stereotypical view of what makes a great leader and tells us it's okay to be different. The experiences she has collated, together with her analysis of the lessons we can learn from them, make *The Unexpected Leader* an invaluable resource for teachers, leaders and policy makers alike.

Natalie Perera, Executive Director and Head of Research, Education Policy Institute

THE UNEXPECTED LEADER

Exploring the real nature of values,
authenticity and moral purpose in education

IESHA SMALL

 independent thinking press

First published by
Independent Thinking Press
Crown Buildings, Bancyfelin, Carmarthen, Wales, SA33 5ND, UK
www.independentthinkingpress.com
and
Independent Thinking Press
PO Box 2223, Williston, VT 05495, USA
www.crownhousepublishing.com

Independent Thinking Press is an imprint of Crown House Publishing Ltd.

Edited by Ian Gilbert

British Library of Cataloguing-in-Publication Data
A catalogue entry for this book is available from the British Library.

Print ISBN 978-178135299-1
Mobi ISBN 978-178135314-1
ePub ISBN 978-178135315-8
ePDF ISBN 978-178135316-5

LCCN 2018968080

Printed and bound in the UK by TJ International, Padstow, Cornwall

Preface

I left the hall where the whole staff were attending a training day on our first day back after the summer holidays and went into the car park, where I began to cry uncontrollably. Huge, body-racking sobs. I don't cry very often and it seemed that I did all my crying for the year to that point in one go. I rang my partner and told her that something was wrong, but I wasn't quite sure what. All I can really remember saying is, "I can't do this again … I can't do it again …" as I sat on the curb, distraught and inconsolable. I can't remember much detail of that conversation, but I did try to go back into work later that day, and again the next, and had the exact same reaction for no obvious reason. Just stepping onto the premises seemed to trigger it. It became apparent that I was temporarily not in a fit state to lead a department, let alone teach my classes. In fact, I really shouldn't have been at work at all. Shortly afterwards, I was signed off sick by my doctor. I can look back now and appreciate that this was the start of a major breakdown, which ended up lasting several months, but I don't think I could have identified that at the time. I had permanently left that school by the end of the calendar year.

After my breakdown, I decided that I never wanted to be the cause of anybody I led feeling that way, or experiencing any form of work-related stress, anxiety or depression due to poor management or unrealistic working expectations. I regrouped and found a new school, where I took a sideways move into a similar position as head of maths. I felt trusted, so I took chances and created space for my team to do the same where possible. I was managed well and I learnt how to be a better manager myself. I found ways to reduce my team's workload so that they could concentrate on what was most important, great teaching.

I discovered that I could help people improve their performance without holding a metaphorical stick all the time, and was delighted to uncover the strengths of team members who had previously been underdeveloped or written off. I watched them gain confidence and thrive, as my own confidence also rebuilt. This environment – where I was accountable but trusted, listened to and given autonomy – gave me the building blocks of a more compassionate working philosophy. I was promoted internally but it was on a fixed-term basis – and when that ended, it felt like time to move on, so I took up an assistant head position in a different secondary school in the Home Counties. For a while, things were good, but then they started to unravel again.

It slowly begun to dawn on me that something wasn't quite right. If you'd asked me then, I'm not sure I could have given articulate, specific reasons why I felt the way I did. There was a lot going on in various aspects of my life and, whatever the particulars were, it all added up to me realising that I just wasn't happy.

I remember waking up one day, possibly during February half term, thinking, "If my life were to continue like this for the next five years, would I be happy?"

The answer was a resounding no. The thought made me want to cry.

"What about if it were just for one more year?"

I felt exactly the same sinking feeling. Even the thought of moving schools again and starting the new school year in September somewhere else, but with all aspects of my life as they were, made me feel real despair. Still, I kept going, putting one foot in front of the other because there wasn't anything obviously wrong. I had a nagging feeling that it didn't quite seem like I was going the right way. Like I may have taken a wrong turn or lost my bearings on the map. But the scenery was familiar and other people were telling me that this was the right direction. What was the problem? What was wrong with me?

As I write this preface, I am sitting overlooking my parents-in-law's garden, watching the wind blow through the trees when I look up from my computer screen. My personal life is happy and full of laughter, and the episode that I describe at the start feels like it happened to another person. During the time I spent off work after my breakdown, I slowly started to feel better and slightly less numb, despondent and overwhelmed. This slow process led to me re-evaluating all aspects of my life. To improve my mental health I decided that I needed to be more creative, so I started using photography to tell the stories of ordinary people who have experienced depression in some way. I've always been interested in people's stories, and I began to wonder about the experiences of other school leaders and how they cope with the demands of the job. I got talking to people in my network and soon realised that feelings of being personally out of sync with your working life and with the expectations of others were, sadly, more common than I'd realised. I set out to gather the stories of other leaders that I could identify with in some aspect. In sharing them, I hope to show people that they are not alone, as I have often felt.

It seems only fair that in a book in which each interviewee – each one involved in school leadership – has given me hours of their time to share the highs and lows of their professional and personal selves that I should mirror their generosity and candour by sharing my own journey. This is not a book about having the answers, although you will find insights and advice along the way. None of the leaders here has all the answers, and I certainly don't. You could say that part of the process of writing this book was to help me find some, or at least to help me work out what my next step might look like. I hope that by reading my story, and those of the leaders I interviewed, you will recognise us all as fellow vulnerable travellers and perhaps take away lessons from our collective experience that will help you to lead more effectively, while being unashamedly who you are.

All the interviewees have been very generous in sharing their stories with me to help others in their leadership journeys. Some names in a few of these stories have been substituted with pseudonyms in order to protect either their own privacy or that of other people in their lives.

Acknowledgements

First, thank you to each of the school leaders who agreed to be interviewed for this book. It would not exist without your generosity and honesty. Your stories have helped me and I know that they will help others.

Second, a practical thank you goes to Claire and Chris Nicholls, as well as Steve Powers and Liz Watkins, who kindly provided me with a quiet place in their homes to write the draft which started to look like the finished version of this book, and kept me fed and hydrated at regular intervals as I disappeared into my writing cave. Special thanks also to Ted Reilly and Sarah Hudson for providing a room with a view in principle.

Thank you to Shaun Connell and Niall McDiamid, who have both long been supportive of my photography and helpful sounding boards about visual matters as well as creative sources of inspiration.

I would like to thank everybody who has given me support or opportunities throughout my career and life to date. There are too many people to mention here by name, but know that you have influenced me. William Owusu, you may not think that you are on this list but I'll never forget your kindness at a very difficult time: you helped me to understand how important creativity was to me.

A special shout-out goes to HipHopEd, who were the first network of educators with whom I really felt at home and whose events were where I first started speaking about education and authenticity. Keep up the great work, Darren Chetty, and thanks for your ongoing support and championing.

Caroline Peden-Smith, thanks for thinking that I had something useful to say to the world, even if it took me three years to work out what.

This book has been through many iterations. Thank you, Mel, for listening to my ideas, for reading and proofreading most of the versions, and for keeping the munchlets out of the conservatory when I was trying to stick to my daily writing target. Also a special thank you for being there throughout all of the experiences that have contributed to my journey as an unexpected leader, only some of which have made it into the book.

Anna Trethewey, Claire Nicholls, David McQueen and Mary Myatt, you were the first people who I shared a readable draft of this book with. Thank you for your time, comments and improvements.

I now know that a book, or any major piece of writing, doesn't really become its best without the work of an editor. Loic Menzies, you have made me a better writer via your comments and feedback on my reports and articles at work. Ian Gilbert, you understood who I was trying to help with *The Unexpected Leader* and gave me patient and insightful advice to turn it from a generic leadership book into one that only I could have written. Louise Penny, you helped beat my manuscript into a publishable book even though it was painful for me at times. I have improved as a writer as a result of your input. Thank you to the rest of the team at Crown House Publishing for getting this book off my computer and out into the world.

Special thanks also go to a group of people who will probably never read this book: the young people who have been affected by my teaching and leading. Thanks for the occasional frustration and frequent laughter, and for making the journey worthwhile.

Finally, Elodie, Gabriel and Seren, thanks for just being.

Contents

Introduction

To get my most recent senior leader positon, part of the two-day interview process included something which I could never have prepared for but had, on reflection, been preparing for my whole life.

I had been interviewed by each of the people who would eventually become my colleagues in different combinations and had to do various tasks that tested my suitability as an individual and against other candidates. Then the head, my future boss, invited me into his office. He was there alone and beckoned me to take a seat in a chair opposite him across his huge desk. Behind him, through the first-floor window, I could see the backs of the houses that overlook part of the school grounds. I was nervous and tired.

"Iesha," he said, "tell me about your background. Who are you? What's brought you to this point?"

I was momentarily stunned. That's not the line of questioning I was expecting. Where was, "Describe how you've implemented a whole-school initiative" and other such senior leadership interview classics?

He told me to relax. I thought for a bit and then I just started talking. I told him about my childhood and the importance that my extended family, as economic migrants, had placed on education. I spoke of the opportunities that I had enjoyed as a result of my education and why I'd entered teaching. I spoke of mistakes that I'd made, and learnt from, and what had led to me being sat in that chair, in that school, at that moment.

Later, quite some time after I'd been appointed, my boss told me that what I'd said when it was just the two of us in his office that day was what had sold it for him. I'd already performed well on the other tasks, but my personal story had been the thing that made him want me, specifically, on his team, because

– despite some of our obvious differences – we shared similar beliefs and that's what he thought more important.

* * *

Education is fundamentally a human endeavour. It is about more than exam results and data, it's about people. It's about identifying and cultivating the talents, character and unique attributes of the children and young people in our care and equipping them with the skills and knowledge they'll need to thrive in the world. However, I often fear that, under various pressures, the system is not allowing teachers to develop as happy and rounded people in the same way that we hope our students will. Every teacher will have a story about what drew them into the profession, a personal philosophy about education and different life experiences to date. Every school leader has to work within the system and navigate accountability, the workload, the data, the expectations of others and their own values. This can easily lead to feelings of alienation, conflict and dissonance. Of feeling like an imposter in a role that doesn't quite fit, doesn't quite feel right.

My own sense of professional and personal incongruence has led to me taking time out and making sideways moves within the world of teaching and school leadership at various points in my career. It was what I needed to do to avoid total burnout. Interested in how others may have navigated this, I did what will become a key theme later in the book and reached out to my network.

The nine teachers whose stories are featured here are peers and role models that I have sought out from the north, south, east and west of England. They are all school leaders with a wealth of different experiences, and they are each a little different from how we might expect a leader to be. They are contacts that I have built over my fourteen years of teaching and leading. I want to share their insights with you, as your personal mentors and role models, as you build your own network of people to challenge and inspire you. Through the process of researching and writing this book, and discussing my emerging ideas with my interviewees, I have realised that – while sometimes it might feel like it – I am not alone. If you are reading this, neither are you. I hope our stories may inspire you, teach you or energise you to teach and lead another day.

I have spent my life and career being told that I am different. Sometimes it's a compliment. Sometimes it's not. Sometimes it's neither, just an observation. It can be easy to downplay difference and see it as a barrier. I'm a confident person generally but, on bad days, I used to feel like that about many of the traits that I possess as a leader and as a person. I tried to fit in. Not rock the boat. Live up to someone else's idea of how I should be. But I have learnt that this is the wrong approach. As such, this book is something of a letter to my younger self as it contains stories and advice from experienced leaders that I wish somebody had given me when I started in education. These are now the mantras that I live by:

* Know what makes you different.
* Find out how to use it as a strength.
* Find others who see it as a strength.
* Use your uniqueness to add value.

In various ways my interviewees epitomise these principles. They are leaders who think differently, just like you. Sometimes their colleagues have advised them to tone down aspects of themselves in order to be more successful – whatever successful means. They might listen respectfully, but they are mindful of when and in what ways they are unwilling to compromise their own values and integrity. In sharing their stories, I hope to offer a connection to the ideas of like-minded people within education. To show that there is room for diversity of thought, approach and opinion in schools. This book draws on my experiences and wider reading, as well as what these school leaders have to say about authenticity, effectiveness and a life well lived. It combines my interest in education with my love of photography, creativity and understanding other people. In reading it, I hope that you better understand your own story and are able to use it positively to inform your future path and find your best fit.

The leaders featured in this book are each unique in their own way and they have been successful in education at different levels. However, this is far from a collection of tales of infallible superheads who are afraid to admit their own humanity. They have all been open and generous in sharing times when they have made mistakes or failed. Their honesty, candidness and vulnerability has been humbling and, in my eyes, brave. I hope that I have done their stories justice by being equally brave when telling my own, which I offer alongside theirs in each chapter.

These leaders do have something in common, however: each has a very clear personal story about what drew them to teaching. Many had clear reasons about why they now lead in particular types of schools, with particular types of students. Hearing them share this was very powerful. It's not something that many people reflect on, especially at the start of their careers when it's natural to focus on the day-to-day demands of the role, but all of the most impressive and socially minded leaders I've met inside, and outside, education have had very clear reasons why they:

* do *what* they do
* do it *where* they do
* do it *how* they do

Knowing yourself well and finding an organisation which allows you to live out your values seems to be an important common key to success. Before we begin to explore how each of these leaders has sought to do this, let me start by telling you a little more about myself.

When you are a class teacher or a middle manager you might expect that being a senior leader will bring you the freedom to do what you want. But a particular role might not be the same in every school, even if the title is. Your actual experience of the role will depend on the school, the ethos and the people. Sometimes, even the same role in the same school can be experienced differently by different people. Our roles are shaped by more than job descriptions, they are shaped by our colleagues and by the working environment. Why am I going into this when I said I was going to tell you about myself? Well, when I became a senior leader, it wasn't what I thought it would be.

Having previously enjoyed a year-long combined role as a head of maths and assistant head, I made the move to another school to take up a permanent assistant headship role. There I experienced what I felt was less freedom and less autonomy. It felt odd and ultimately made me very unhappy. Now, in real terms, this may not have actually been as bad as it appeared to be at the time. I had a wonderful working relationship with my boss, who I respect and am still on good terms with. It's easy to blame external circumstances – like the government's accountability measures, a school's lack of freedom, or the culture within a senior leadership team (SLT) – but with maturity and experience you realise that things are never black and white. External factors can and do play a part but we also have individual agency, even if, as the actress Michaela Coel says, "the *only* power we have, is the power to say 'no'".[1] I've since reflected that how I felt inside probably made me act in ways that didn't help the situations I was finding frustrating, and I'd want to do things differently now. In any case, there was definitely a change in my own self-perception which I'd never really experienced before.

I think that because I felt stifled, in time it became a self-fulfilling prophecy. I stifled myself with my actions and limited my own capabilities. As a normally confident person, I felt my confidence and self-esteem related to work slowly depleting. I stopped talking freely and stopped doing the things that made me desirable and hireable in the first place. I used to write a thoughtful, and occasionally controversial, blog. It allowed me space to reflect and to explore ideas about education and about my own practice. Suddenly I felt I couldn't do that any more. But why? Nobody had ever said anything to me – definitely not my boss – it just didn't feel safe for me to express ideas that could be interpreted in different ways or that were complicated or conflicted. So I stopped writing.

Until I began this book, that is – at which point I also decided to take a break from school leadership. I found a role that allows me to continue to make a difference to society and to effect social change but via the lens of policy, research and

---

1 Broadcasters, Michaela Coel: MacTaggart Lecture in Full, *Broadcast Now* (23 August 2018). Available at: https://www.broadcastnow.co.uk/broadcasters/michaela-coel-mactaggart-lecture-in-full/5131910.article.

working with decision makers. For two years after resigning, I still taught two days a week at the school where I was an assistant head. The decision to leave was voluntary and amicable. It was what I needed to do for myself at that time. I still have no idea if I will ever return to school leadership.

As an associate at a think tank, my specialist area is young people, education and leadership – basically working towards creating a fairer society. I still feel like I'm making a difference, just from an alternative perspective. I've gone from feeling like I wasn't fit to do anything to having interesting discussions with CEOs, ministers and policy makers and being invited to give my opinion on various topics that matter to me. More importantly, I have a more flexible way of working that means I can regularly work from home and see my young family a bit more, while still feeling intellectually challenged.

Now that I am no longer a school leader, I feel free to write about school leadership again. So this book is for anyone like me who feels they don't quite fit the mould or is struggling to find a way forward within the system. It's me lighting a flare to guide you to other education professionals who have found a way to have different perspectives and approaches, while still being effective and having an impact on their schools, their departments and the children and communities that they serve. It's a chance for the younger me, and the current you, to learn from my mistakes and to see what I have learnt and would do differently. It's a snapshot of a particular period of my professional life alongside key lessons and ideas to implement from each of the school leaders featured.

Each chapter starts by inviting you to consider your own circumstances and feelings, before my own experience is briefly outlined so you know you aren't alone. This is followed by an exploration of the leadership journey of a school leader, compiled from an interview in their own words, featuring key episodes that explore what they have experienced, what they have learnt and how they have taken ownership of their professional and personal lives. Then we delve into what you and I can learn from each leader, to guide us as we each pursue our own onward journey. The chapter ends with a final message or thought from the school leader in question.

The Unexpected Leader is organised into three parts. Part I: Circumstances explores our readiness for the leadership roles that we may find ourselves in, our fears around lack of experience and, for many of us, imagined imposter syndrome. Part II: Humanity considers the impact of our personality and core values on our roles and actions as school leaders. And finally, Part III: Beyond looks at the impact of personal lives on our working lives and vice versa, as well as how we can look after ourselves mentally while being effective school leaders, as well as the dangers if we don't. The book ends with a summary of the recurring themes which came out strongly during all of the interviews, and some final resources from me that I hope will help you in a more practical way if particular themes from the book resonate with you.

So, this is the end of a particular chapter in life and career for me but hopefully the start of one for you, my reader. There is a way to work within the system, take care of yourself and remain true to who you are. There is wisdom in every chapter of this book from people who, on the surface, may or may not appear to be like you but on a deeper level are: whether in position, title, beliefs, personality, approach or stage in life. You will see that you are not alone. You may be unexpected, an oddity, a maverick or whatever word is applied to you in your organisation or working environment. You may feel alone in your school but there will be fellow outliers in your borough, county or academy chain.

The thing that really matters is understanding what makes you unique, owning it and using it to make a difference to improving the quality of people's lives. You do not need to apologise for who you are. Read how I and others have done it and learn from our experiences to decide how leading authentically looks for you. This book is me trying to make sense of working and leading in education. If I can help you to find a way to make a difference in your own world while being more authentically yourself then it will have been worth it.

Read. Reflect. Ponder. But, most importantly, act. Then share and inspire other educators to do things in their own way to benefit all our young people; proudly, humbly, unashamedly and, crucially, collaboratively.

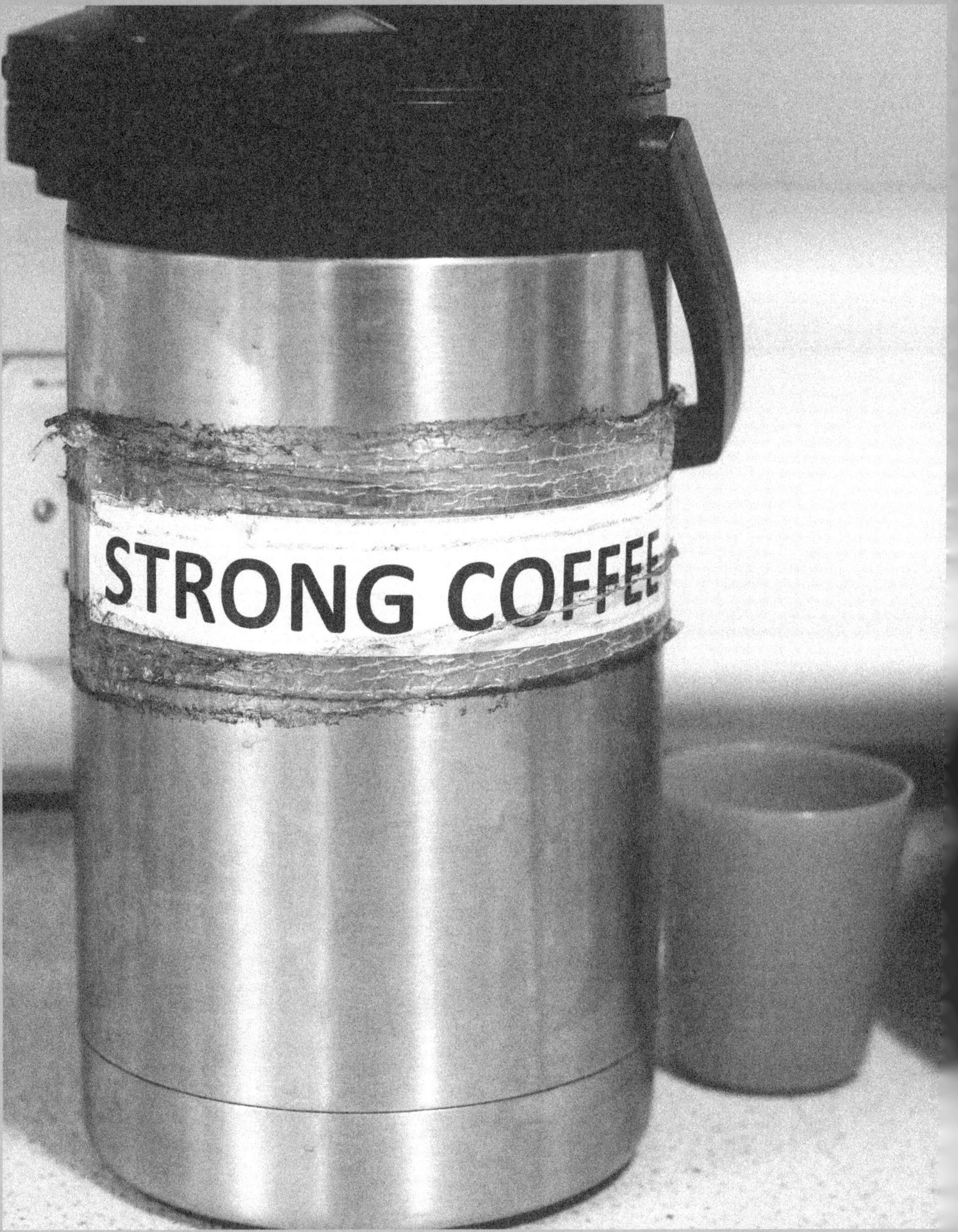
STRONG COFFEE

PART I

CIRCUMSTANCES

Circumstances

We don't always choose to be leaders, occasionally leadership chooses us. A sudden departure, a temporary absence, a boss' recommendation for a new role or some other unplanned circumstance, all of these can cause us to suddenly find ourselves filling leadership shoes when we weren't even expecting to try them on. I used to think that the skills and behaviours of leaders were fixed, but I've changed my thinking to see that leadership is in fact situational – and sometimes the situation chooses us, rather than the other way around. At times like these we may not feel ready to take on a role, we secretly wish we had a little more time to hone our craft, but we can find a way to adapt and be effective if we are willing to learn from our own experiences and those of others.

CHAPTER 1

I felt like an imposter
– Leah's story

"It was partly the feeling of being thrust into the situation without any preparation. The worry and fear of doing the wrong thing."

You

﹡ Have you ever been asked to perform a role that you had no intention of applying for?

﹡ Perhaps you have been asked to fill a role because one of your colleagues is on maternity leave?

﹡ Perhaps somebody has left unexpectedly and you've been asked to step in until a replacement is found?

﹡ Perhaps there was an expected departure but the vacancy has taken longer than expected to fill?

﹡ You are the best available fit, or at least everybody else seems to think so.

﹡ So you agree to do the role, but then what?

In these situations it's easy to feel like an imposter because, well, you pretty much are. It's not even your real job. Taking on a new role is always challenging but it's especially tough if you've been asked to step up suddenly or before you feel ready and skilled enough to do so. I know because this has happened to me. It's not the same as when you've actively applied for a job. In those situations there is often a preparation period, even if only in your own head. You know that you'll be doing something different, so you start to mentally prepare yourself and possibly gather advice from other people in similar roles. If you are really lucky, you may even get a formal handover period.

Whatever the circumstances, the point is, the job needs to be done and you are expected to do it. Sometimes, just to keep things extra fun, you may even have to do your normal job at the same time. If you are anything like me, you won't just want to be a caretaker, you'll want to do it well, to prove to yourself that you are capable. Will it be stressful? Initially, yes. Feel like grappling in the dark? Absolutely. However, acting or temporary positions can be an excellent learning experience and a real chance to test your capabilities. You can come out stronger, wiser and a better professional. You could even come out with a permanent promotion or a new role.

Me

Early in my career, I never wanted to be a leader. I was a maths teacher and really enjoyed my subject. Two or three years in, I thought I was getting pretty good at teaching, or at least being less crap! The kids were understanding what I was teaching. I was more confident. I was becoming trusted. I'd even helped to train some other teachers and had taken on some extra responsibility. This was in my very first school, a large comprehensive in Islington, North London, where I trained as part of the Teach First scheme, which was then in its second year.[1] I was part of a wonderful department with an innovative and creative head of subject who seemed to love her job and led a very happy team.

Moving to a new school, I found things a little different. I looked around at the heads of department and they seemed, well, how can I put it? Stressed. And under pressure. Especially those leading the core subjects: English, maths and science. If middle leadership looked like this, I wasn't sure it was what I wanted. Being an SLT member wasn't even on my radar. When I did see them, they seemed pretty stressed too and there appeared to be cliques within the team which got in the way of what the school seemed to need. I looked at what I was meant to see as my next step and was distinctly underwhelmed.

I was, however, somebody who wanted a challenge and wanted to grow. Some may see it as a strength, others as a character flaw, but standing still has never really been an option for me. In fact, it can feel like going backwards. Disillusioned with what I'd seen of leadership, I decided that I wanted to be an advanced skills teacher (AST). A governmental education improvement strategy, the idea was that great teachers who wanted to remain in the classroom could earn nationally recognised accreditation. They would still teach but with a reduced timetable which would allow them to spend time helping other teachers – both within and beyond their school – to improve. It sounded like the perfect fit for me: challenge, teaching the subject I love, and time to work with and develop other teachers. Sign me up!

---

1   Teach First is an education charity founded in London in 2003. It is now national and self-describes as a scheme that "provides world-class teacher and leadership training for people who are passionate about giving children from the poorest backgrounds a great education". See www.teachfirst.org.

A year into role in my second school, I was doing fine. I'd had some opportunities to develop professionally and was still planning my route to AST-dom. I had been really happy at my first school but it was a comprehensive for 11- to 16-year-olds, which meant only teaching up to GCSE. I really wanted the opportunity to teach A level, which is why I had left. That's where the proper maths starts, I thought. Calculus to the left and right, my friends. One evening I bumped into a deputy head from that first school. She had since moved on somewhere else, as had our former head teacher, who she said I should call. Like the curious young woman I was – I am now slightly less young but just as curious – I did. He told me that he was now running a school in challenging circumstances and could do with a deputy head of maths. Would I like to join his team?

Still curious, I said yes. However, when I started, things were a bit more challenging than I'd realised I was letting myself in for. The head of maths, to whom I'd just become deputy, was under siege because GCSE results had been very low for some time. The SLT wanted fast improvements and he appeared to be under a lot of pressure. I say appeared to be because I didn't really get the chance to get to know him. I can't remember the exact timescales, but within probably about half a term of me joining the school he suddenly went off sick. One day he was there; the next, without warning, he wasn't.

So I became acting head of maths. With less than two months' experience as a deputy, I would be leading a subject in which the results were expected to jump significantly – by double-digit percentage points – that summer, in a department that had been historically underperforming in a school regularly at the bottom of the borough's league tables. I had no idea what I was doing. But I didn't have time to think about that. I had to lead the department, provide stability and ensure that every single one of the hundreds of students at the school got the best maths education my team could offer them. At least until a replacement head could be found.

When writing a book called *The Unexpected Leader*, I knew that I had to have a chapter that took the title literally – for people who, like me, had not initially set out to take on a role but were forced to due to circumstance. This is an experience shared by Leah, currently a deputy head teacher in a large inner-city primary school. Leah is a family friend who also happens to be a teacher. We've known each other for about fifteen years and we started teaching at roughly the same time. Her story takes us to when she was working as an assistant head and quite suddenly, due to a number of unexpected factors, found herself as joint acting head. Like me, she found a way to inhabit this imposter role and became a better professional as a result. I hope Leah's story offers anyone who is suddenly acting in a leadership positon many actionable points to take away, as well as the knowledge that you are not alone in how you feel.

Leah

Even before becoming acting head, Leah had moments of feeling like an imposter as an SLT member:

> "I think when I first started, I felt kind of buoyant and cheered on by the fact that I'd got the job in the first place. I had lots of energy and things I wanted to try. There are times as well when you start in a leadership position and you feel like a bit of a fraud. Like somebody's going to come and knock on your door and say, 'Um, what are you doing? Get out.' Especially as people don't trust you innately, just because you are an SLT member. It took a long time, at least a term, for others in the team to believe that what I had to say was worth listening to or to respect me, and rightly so. You don't just respect somebody who walks in and says, 'I've got this label.' That's fair enough. So in the beginning, I felt like I had to fake it till I made it. I wanted to do well, I wanted to learn."

The initial support of the then head made the process easier:

> "My boss was very skilled at helping to grow people. I'd never experienced that before. In my previous setting, everyone was lovely but there was very little leadership support or development in that sense. Right from the word

go, in our one to ones, I'd leave feeling inspired. She knew a lot about leadership. She's read a lot, she introduced me to books that I should read and straight away I was learning new things. She's quite an inspiring leader herself; done a lot in her life and changed a lot in the school. I started right at the bottom of the leadership scale. I had no experience, so every year she'd build up my appraisal process and give me something new to try, even if it was just dipping my feet in."

Having enjoyed this structure and support within the school previously, suddenly being thrust into the joint head role without warning was all the harder:

"Although we knew the head was sick, we didn't know when she was coming back … there was no information coming from the top down. There was an awful lot going on in the school; it was an Ofsted window, and we were dealing with some quite contentious parental complaints. Because there were no other layers of leadership to take things to, that was very challenging. I think our whole problem with it was not knowing. We were never told whether she'll be back in a week or whether she'll be back in a month. The weeks went on. We were looking at each other saying, 'Shall we defer Ofsted? Will they expect to see the head teacher? I think we could do it without her but I don't know.'"

The lack of information and the unpredictability of the situation compounded the day-to-day issues that Leah and her co-head were dealing with:

"My role had gone from something that was incredibly structured, like I was saying, all of those systems, always knowing what was coming up. Well calendared. Knowing the challenge you've taken on. Suddenly I was being faced with day-to-day challenges and going back to that feeling of being a bit out of your depth that maybe you experience when you start the job. It's not that my fellow acting head and I weren't used to challenges, it's not that we weren't used to being in leadership positions. I knew that I was capable

but there was a fear that came with unexpectedly being at the top of the chain of command. There was nowhere else to go and we were accountable for everything, suddenly. I didn't have that nice structured build-up that had happened for the rest of my career."

Early on, Leah faced a particularly difficult situation following an incident involving a parental argument in the playground which resulted in the police being called:

"Usually there are enough layers of leadership, and formalities and protocols that work, but because some of those layers had been removed and we were only acting as head, it was quite challenging. We were both so stressed because things were being thrown at us left, right and centre. We just found it really intimidating. We were taking minutes in meetings, we were doing everything very formally but it was quite stressful, to the point where we were going home and not sleeping and feeling really worried about what was going to happen in this situation."

As the situation worsened, asking for external help proved to be the best solution:

"In the end we rang the head of school improvement and asked him to come in as a kind of independent witness in a meeting because the parents were getting more aggressive and it was going nowhere. That had quite a positive impact and we were glad we did it. But I think you don't really know what help to ask for sometimes. You don't want to be seen as being weak. He was lovely and supportive and everything was fine. I think in hindsight, now, that was so ridiculous. But at the time it was all-encompassing. I thought, 'It's never going to be over. I can't sleep. This is really stressful. I'm not eating properly. I'm worried about coming to work and dealing with this stuff.' Within weeks it was like it had never happened, it had died down and everything was fine. The school just kept rolling and I was thinking, 'Why did I give it that much energy?'"

Hindsight is a wonderful thing but this experience also gave Leah deeper insights that she'll carry with her into the future:

> "I think that taught me a lesson. I need to not catastrophise things. No matter how unexpected or stressful something is, it doesn't mean that I can't deal with it. I just need to be a little bit more reflective and calm. I remember one of the governors saying, 'You will come out the other side of this and realise how much you've learnt.' She was completely right. I look at it now and think, 'What was the good of being that stressed about it?' The school's still running. We're still in our jobs. Everybody's fine. Nobody died! It was partly the feeling of being thrust into the situation without any preparation. At the time, it was new and scary. The worry and fear of doing the wrong thing all contributed to the stress, but actually, now, I know I did the right thing. I can do it, and I'd do it again."

Change and development take time but trying to influence cultural shifts in the school made Leah realise how much she's grown both personally and professionally:

> "When I first started at the school it was a very closed environment. If you walked into someone's classroom as an SLT member, they would ask, 'Can I help you?' Teachers were very fearful of people coming in and watching them teach: it was all formal observation. We've now moved to a really open-door culture where learning walks are common and people go around and look at each other's practice. We do a lot of peer observations through the teacher learning community. It's all part of the embedded culture. It's taken time to build that up. I had led INSETs before as a middle leader but now when I run training sessions I feel that I'm talking from a position of authority. 'This is what I've researched. This is what I know. Here is the relevant educational literature.' I feel like through doing that, I have the confidence to stand in front of people and share that with them. I realised, a year into my master's, that I am actually quite knowledgeable about this. I've gone from a point where I felt a bit of a fraud when I started in senior leadership to knowing

something useful. I've still got a hell of a lot to learn but I know that I've got something valuable to give and that I've developed an expertise within the school that I can share with people. We've done big pieces of work around resilience and mindsets and seen it have a really positive impact in the school. That's been done through a system of teacher learning communities that I set up and by changing the culture of the school as a whole. I think little 22-year-old teacher me who had locked herself in the toilet would never have thought that I could change the mindset of a whole school and help over 400 children to develop these skills. I just never would have thought that I could do that. It's interesting when you think about it like that. Things happen slowly over time, but when you look at it from then to now, you realise the amount of progress you've made."

What can we learn from Leah's story?

* Ask for help

It's fine to ask for help. As Leah says:

"Seeing how supportive and non-judgemental the borough were, I realised it was fine to ask them for help because we were in a unique situation. Now I know other young heads and older heads who I have developed relationships with over time. Having had that experience, I wouldn't hesitate to call someone up and go, 'What have you done in this situation?'"

I have heard this from school leaders time and time again and it echoes my own experience. It's okay to ask for help, there will always be somebody who is willing. In Chapter 2, we'll meet Ben, an inexperienced assistant head, who explains how he asked a peer on his SLT to be an informal mentor for a few months. Allana, a head teacher who we'll meet in Chapter 7, is adamant in her belief that the help and support of her professional network beyond her school is what enabled her to remain in leadership after a potentially career-ending experience.

Often, asking somebody in a comparable position is a good place to start. Overwhelmingly, most people want to help. School leaders of all types generally remember how hard it was when they first started and will want to help you succeed. If there is nobody in your own school you feel you can approach, then ask around in your borough or multi-academy trust (MAT). There will be other people in a similar situation who you can talk to. Lila, a head teacher whose story is explored in Chapter 3, explained that having fellow heads, with whom she shared an ethos and could use as a sounding board, in her MAT was invaluable in her early years in the role. There will be local networks or meetings that people in similar roles attend. Why not sound a few people out informally at the end of one of those? My experience has been that people are incredibly generous and I have, in turn, helped others when they have reached out to me, even if I didn't previously know them.

✳ Look after your mental health

Being placed in an unexpected situation, possibly for an undetermined time period, can be a very stressful experience. You naturally want to do a good job but your number one priority is to keep yourself healthy and functioning in all ways. Initially, Leah's situation took its toll on her:

> "I went to go and talk to somebody because I felt like I was on the verge of something. I was feeling very stressed to the point where … it was making me physically ill. Lack of sleep, not eating properly, physical symptoms of feeling very anxious and nauseous on the way to work and all this stuff, and I knew that this wasn't healthy. So I went to see a doctor and they were very supportive. It was calming, it was kind of cathartic, talking about it out loud. Just by hearing somebody say, 'It's going to be alright. It's going to get better,' I was like, 'Yeah, you're right, it's the situation.' I think after that happened I felt more in control. It really made me reflect on the fact that I live in the first world. I have a roof over my head. I'm very fortunate. I have a loving family and husband and friends that are amazing. I should not be in

a position where I go to work and I feel that stressed and negative. It made me more protective of myself. It made me think, 'I'm not going to just blindly take any promotion that comes my way in the future. I'm going to think about whether that's the right choice for me.'"

Other leaders that I interviewed also mentioned the importance of noticing signs that their role was impacting their health and wellbeing. This is especially prominent in Scarlet's story, told in Chapter 9.

✳ Give yourself time to reflect

It can feel like everything needs an answer or decision now. It doesn't.

> *"You don't have to respond right this second. If you are anxious or panicky, give yourself time to reflect and come back when you are feeling more rational."*

This is excellent advice from Leah. You don't need to have all the answers immediately and it's almost always a mistake to respond when you are in a heightened emotional state. Earlier in my career, I was known for being good at my job but a bit of a hothead; I share one memorable example in Chapter 8. Sure, this was often because I felt that colleagues had initially not behaved in the best way but my response didn't always cover me in glory. With time, experience and maturity, I have found that sometimes excusing myself from a situation, giving myself time to reflect and responding when the emotion is less raw is the best way to deal with things. Or sometimes it's worth seeking a second opinion.

✳ You will come out the other side of adversity

It may not feel like it now, but this will pass. It's an incredible learning experience. If you are ambitious, consider it a secondment or even an extended job interview, a chance to really show what you can do. Even if the experience makes you decide that you don't want to take the next step just yet, you'll still learn so much that will help you understand your normal job from a different perspective when you return to it. With hindsight, Leah reflected positively upon her experience of being acting head teacher:

> "I think it was a success. The school kept running. It was a difficult year but actually there were no big issues. There were no parents going, 'Where the hell is the head teacher? What the hell is going on?' The children were still making great progress. There was still great teaching. The systems were still working and we kept running, and that was really positive."

When I asked her if she would apply for headship now she told me:

> "At first I felt, no way! There's no way I'm putting myself in that position. Now, on reflection, I realise I probably have a lot to offer. I also know that because of the kind of person I am, I'd probably be really good at it. That may sound arrogant but I work hard and I know I'd give it my all. It's just about whether I'm in the right place, in the right stage of my career."

My own experience was that I did grow into the role that I suddenly had to fill. I had a wonderful department who put up with my mistakes while learning on the job because they could see that, ultimately, I really cared. The team got behind me and maths results jumped significantly that year. The head teacher decided that I had done a good job and opted not to advertise externally. I was offered the role permanently. I accepted, having realised that I could have impact over a larger number of students in a leadership position and that there were many elements of the role that I enjoyed. It also seemed I had some aptitude for it; I realised that I could do the job at least as well as other heads of department, and in some cases better.

Parting words

But of course our working lives are only one aspect of our formative experience. Leah also told me about the major life events that have shaped her personally and professionally:

> *"The death of my mum really changed me as a person. I think that really defined who I was in my early twenties. I moved to London. I tried new things. Very soon after that I met my first husband. I realise now in hindsight that a lot of the things I did in my relationship were for him. Going into leadership happened after our marriage breakdown. It was something I'd worked towards. It was all my doing. Out of that came positives. I don't have any regrets."*

Earlier in my career, I tried to completely compartmentalise my professional and personal life. In reality that's impossible, how you feel about one affects the other. A chance encounter with a former classmate made Malcolm, an assistant head we'll meet in Chapter 5, leave his corporate career to start teaching. For Allana, in Chapter 7, it was her mother's terminal illness that made her reconsider her working life.

If you have had personal challenges, think about the fact that you are still here, that you learnt from them and that they are now in the past. Whatever happens when you take on a role you aren't quite ready for, you will come out the other side. Then it will just be one of those things that happened and made you who you are. As Leah says:

> *"Realise what you're capable of. Advice I'd give to myself now would be to think about how much you've gone through in your life. No matter how catastrophic and hideous something is, there is another side. There is calm water again."*

CHAPTER 2

I don't have enough experience – Ben's story

"I wonder whether I'm always going to have this inferiority complex."

You

* Perhaps you see a new role advertised internally or elsewhere. At first you think you can do it. But there is a nagging feeling.

* Perhaps you've been teaching for a relatively short time compared to others in your school or wider professional network.

* Perhaps you are fairly young compared to others you see in similar roles.

* What if people don't take you seriously?

* What if you aren't that good?

* Are you too inexperienced?

* Let's say you get the job. Great!

* Only what if you get found out?

* What if your internal naysayer is right?

In careers outside of education, fast-track paths – where promising candidates are given a wide range of experiences and promoted to senior positions in a relatively short period of time – are not unusual. Teaching, however, can take a more traditional approach to career advancement. You do one role for a suitable amount of time then you go onto the next rung of the ladder for another and, if it's what you are interested in doing, you make your slow and clearly laid out ascent. Sometimes there can be a sense of biding your time and paying your dues. Generally, reaching senior positions takes some time. The vast majority of school leaders are over 40 according to figures from the Department for Education (DfE), with roughly 60% of deputies and assistants and over 85% of heads falling into this demographic.[1]

---

1 Department for Education, School Workforce in England: November 2017. Tables: School Workforce Census 2017 (28 June 2018). Available at: https://www.gov.uk/government/statistics/school-workforce-in-england-november-2017. These percentages are extrapolated from the data in Table 4.

Me

I read mechanical engineering at university and spent a year as a graduate engineer before deciding that it wasn't the career for me and becoming a teacher. During my year working as a fleet engineer for a train operating company, I led and directed the work of engineers many years older than me. I was the youngest teacher in the first maths department I led. I was also the youngest member of both SLTs that I've been part of. I've had to lead and line manage people who could have been my teacher when I was at school, sometimes who could have taught my parents. It isn't necessarily right or well-founded, but we do tend to form judgements about competence based on factors like age. I have at times certainly felt that older colleagues were looking at me like I had something to prove.

Generally, I'm a confident person, especially when I know I can take an approach that has worked out well before. But senior leadership isn't like that. Often there are one-off projects to deliver or situations you face that may be different to anything else you've ever experienced. At times I have felt like an imposter. At times I have been acutely aware of people saying negative things because they feel like they should have been the one to get the job, irrespective of whether they were brave enough to actually apply for it. Sometimes my self-doubt has stopped me from applying for positions that I know I have the skills for, I'm well-qualified enough to do and that others who are more experienced than me and who I trust professionally feel I would be good at.

Ben

Ben's story resonated with me. At the time of our interview, he was under thirty and had been in post as an assistant head teacher at a school in the south-west of England for under a year. Ben teaches Spanish and was the first in his family to go to university, where he read law. In the final year of his degree he started to become disillusioned with his legal studies and got involved with a summer school, teaching teenagers from the Welsh valleys. This experience made him decide that teaching was the right career for him. He didn't entirely leave his degree behind because his favourite topic to teach as part of the Spanish curriculum is human rights, which he believes makes "students aware, critical and more empathetic". Ben's students would describe him as "principled, sassy and enthusiastic". Ben believes that education is transformative and that school leadership is about "fighting for the voiceless and vulnerable".

Ben is someone who is well respected by colleagues and good at his job. When I did some long-term coaching at his school, several members of staff made unsolicited comments about how good he was and how he had helped them. Yet Ben still doubts himself, as do many leaders, irrespective of age or gender. His first experience of leadership was as maternity cover for the head of Spanish. He reflected on the advice he was given by colleagues at the time:

> "I got offered the head of Spanish position as maternity cover in my second full year of teaching, and I was directly promoted over the other Spanish teacher in the department. I felt like I was really inexperienced. 'Why should I do this? Who am I to go in there?' I only did it because somebody said to me, 'You should go for this, Ben. You can do it now or you can do it in ten years' time.' Obviously self-doubt came in anyway. I thought I could do it because I know, or I thought I knew, how to lead people and hopefully inspire them and get them moving in the right direction and I just thought to myself, 'I've seen so many teachers who are ineffective and yet they are leading because they are the last person left.' I thought I could do some good. People were saying, 'You've got the potential to do this, so do it. Why waste your time?' These days, I would always say to people in the same situation, do it now. If an opportunity comes up, take it now because you'll learn."

Ben had been in post as head of faculty in a new school for a relatively short time when the opportunity to become an assistant head teacher came up as a temporary post. Once again, trusted colleagues thought he should apply, and this time he had learnt from his previous experience:

> "When the assistant head for teaching and learning job came up, I said, 'I just don't know if I'm ready for this. I don't know if I'm doing well enough

in my current job as head of department.' My colleague said, 'Look, you can do this job, just go for it.' I went for it and I got it. I've always felt that I've been inexperienced, throughout my career, because I consider myself to always be learning. I get to a point where I don't necessarily know if I'm doing the right thing. I've kind of always wondered, 'Could I break this? Is it all going to fall apart?' I'll often watch other members of the SLT and learn from what they are doing as well. So I wonder whether I'm always going to have this inferiority complex."

Ben believes that it's important for staff to have the freedom to try things out as we can only learn from doing, as his own experience has shown him. He has tried to use his influence as an SLT member to positively impact the working culture within his school:

"I think it's really important for teachers to be empowered and happy. We are constantly referred to as a profession but I don't necessarily think schools actually treat people like professionals. I think they treat them, occasionally, like petulant children. If you really want people to be engaged with how well they are teaching and the impact their actions are having, you need staff to be empowered. To have choices. To have a voice. To be able to consider and defend their work.

"For example, think of a lesson observation. That is just one person's opinion of what is going on in a lesson. If I came in and watched it, the most important thing is coming out afterwards and asking the teacher, 'What did you think about that?' Because that can hugely sway a judgement. That teacher knows the students in that room and we need to be aware of this, and of their insights. By giving them empowerment in terms of their practice, they are empowered in their voice. They are empowered in their inclusion in the whole school system. I think it makes for better teaching, for great teaching. More than when people are given resources, told what to deliver and criticised when their marking is wrong. I don't feel that works. Let's get the right people in the right locations and then get out of their way and let

them do what they need to do. Of course we support them when needed but actually, let them do it. Let them try.

"I try to build teachers up within the team. Things like sharing good practice in meetings, nominating staff for hero of the week, getting people's names up there. Bringing them up with the head and being positive. Getting everyone's voice included. I felt if I could bring people along, then I could get them to be invested in themselves a bit more and actually I feel like it has worked. I feel like the positivity in the team is massive compared to when I started. So that's what I'm trying to do. I'm trying to make people feel happy in themselves but also happy to be in the team so they want to do it. That's my experience. You have to think about all of these things as an SLT member because you have a huge amount of power. The power relationship you have in a school is gigantic and your influence can be huge. You need to use that for good and not evil. Think about the power relationship that your position creates, because if you don't you can end up really screwing with people, I think."

Continuous learning has also been essential in Ben's experience, both in terms of shaping and directing his practice and in terms of giving him confidence in his own ability and ideas:

"I've done a master's and that taught me so much about my teaching. I was looking at it in such a critical and analytical way and I still use what I learnt from the course today within my own practice, particularly related to how I structure learning and how I engage students, so I found that really useful. Further study has affected my leadership, not necessarily in my style but in my ability to stand back and say, 'You know what, this is proven, I've thought about it and I'm not doing a knee-jerk here. I've looked at this and I've assessed it and I've considered it.' I think that's really helped me and my confidence. I'm doing a doctorate at the moment, partly because I like the challenge and I like to feel like I'm thinking. I like that pain you feel when you think. Also this doctorate has taught me how to research even further. I've

now developed in terms of doing research in school, I know how to critically look at policy, education policy as a whole, and relate that to whole-school policy. I think my doctoral studies have made me that bit more considered. I think that's a really powerful skill."

When I asked Ben about his colleagues' perceptions of him given his relatively young age, he said:

"I haven't had a huge amount of issues with people going, 'Well, he's only been doing it this amount of time' to my face. I don't talk about my academic study that often in school but people know about it. I've been able to put some aspects of teaching and learning forward across the school and I feel that the knowledge from my research is probably one of the things that pulls into that. I think it does back up my ideas and initiatives. When I first became an assistant head, part of the school restructuring meant that I was also head of history, geography, ethics and Spanish. I was suddenly the head of a massive department, with the most teachers in the entire school. I felt so inexperienced. My big issue and my big worry was because I'm not a subject specialist, how do I lead? I think that taught me the importance of speaking authentically, and I spent time researching it. How could I make myself authentic as a leader? Part of that was creating a vision, it was about bringing everyone together, sharing practice and also knowing enough about the specification and the subjects that are being taught to be able to actively lead."

What can we learn from Ben's story?

* Always keep learning

Ben has a love of learning. It's helped him to negotiate situations that he hasn't encountered before and to compensate for feelings of inexperience. For him, leaders should continually learn and not let the day-to-day demands of being on the SLT stop that:

> "Think about your SLT and meetings, there is so much firefighting isn't there? Your professional learning can really come to the back of that but books allow me to connect to something. It's that innate desire to learn that made me want to be a teacher in the first place."

For Ben, learning is about more than becoming a better professional himself. He sees it as part of a wider duty that helps with his own mission:

> "The point is empowering people, isn't it? Education empowers. By constantly learning as leaders you're empowering yourself to deal with situations better. To be able to inspire people more, and then you're empowering kids to live their lives. Some people forget that. If you stop learning, what's the point?"

Ben has chosen to learn in a formalised way via his master's and PhD, but this may not be for everybody. After five years of study which resulted in my master's in engineering, the idea of another course of formalised learning brings me out in a cold sweat. During our interview, Ben also mentioned several books that have influenced him professionally. A potentially surprising influence was the comedian Tina Fey's *Bossypants*, which taught him how to implement initiatives in the face of obstacles and influenced his thinking about leaders needing to "get the right people in the right locations and then get out of their way and let them do what they need to do".[2] The journey that eventually led to me writing this book started with me teaching myself to become a better photographer. Choose what interests you and delve deeper. It can be via a formal course or via self-directed learning. As teachers, we constantly expect students to learn so it seems only fair that we should be constantly learning too. The theme of continuous learning recurred in conversations I had with various other interviewees. Incidentally, it's what movie

---

2 Tina Fey, *Bossypants* (London: Sphere, 2011).

executive Barry Diller says has been key to his varied and successful career, and in interviews he has identified himself as an "infinite learner".[3]

✳ Reflect on skills you have learnt in previous roles that can help you in new, unfamiliar positions

You may be worried about your ability to do this new role, but you will have had successes in your career so far and there will be elements that you can learn from. You are never entirely starting from zero. Ben reflected on the roles that he had held before becoming an assistant head and realised that he had learnt something significant from each:

> *"I did a previous job called lead teacher and that was basically about coaching staff. I learnt how to have difficult conversations. That role taught me to be compassionate and understanding. People were coming to me because they were struggling and had been receiving poor observations. It was about trying to bring these people along and get them really engaged with their practice and thinking about what they were doing, but in a compassionate way. When you think about it, you realise that all your experiences to date have been building up your skills and even in your current role there will always be new situations to face. As an SLT member, I think you should be learning but I also think you should engage your own learning. It's fundamental. It doesn't have to be massive things. It could be how to run a meeting to time. If anyone knows that, please let me know! New areas will always appear and may seem daunting at first, like the first time I excluded a student and the first time I had to do a parent meeting. First time I had to stand up and do a staff training session solo. First SLT meeting to a certain extent. But every time I do something new I think, 'Okay, I can do this now and I've got better simply because of doing it.'"*

---

3 Barry Diller quoted in Reid Hoffman, Infinite Learner, *Masters of Scale*, episode 14 [podcast]. Available at: https://mastersofscale.com/barry-diller-infinite-learner-2/.

✳ Find somebody more experienced to be your sounding board

I have been extremely lucky to have had a number of unofficial and more formal coaches and mentors throughout my life and career. As a middle leader, I used to have a regular peer coaching session with two other heads of department in my school. Later, as a senior leader, I had a half-termly coaching session with the head teacher of a local school, which I'd specifically requested as part of my professional development. In *Real Artists Don't Starve*, the writer Jeff Goins explores the concept of being an apprentice in order to become skilled at a craft.[4] Being a leader is not exactly the same as being a master craftsman, but to become skilled in any role theoretical learning can only take you so far. At some point you also need to stop reading books, going to conferences or talking to people and you need to start taking action. Your on-the-job learning can be accelerated and supported by having a mentor or coach, so find someone to apprentice yourself to. Ben talked about the value he found in being mentored for three months when he first became an assistant head teacher:

> *"Having a mentor was really useful because it opened my eyes up to a way of managing and leading which was completely different to my own. Being mentored allowed me to tap into someone else's experience. I would advise finding a mentor because it just gets you thinking. You have to present your ideas and experiences to somebody who has never heard them and you make so many links as you do so. You suddenly sit there and go, 'Actually, I've understood this more than I've ever understood it.' That's the way it works for me, anyway.*

> *"I think you have to find someone you respect. I approached my mentor and he was really positive. Sometimes he used our sessions as time to bounce ideas back off me, which was really good. That made me feel kind of legit! Find someone who shares the values you have but maybe approaches them in a different way. You don't want somebody who is going to be sycophantic or*

---

4 Jeff Goins, *Real Artists Don't Starve: Timeless Strategies for Thriving in the New Creative Age* (Nashville, TN: Nelson Books, 2017).

somebody who is only going to perpetuate what you already have. You want somebody who is going to challenge you. Someone who is different to you. Go for someone who has got excellent practice, who is really willing to share, someone who is really willing to give that time to you. You always get those who are easy to notice because they shout the loudest. Sometimes it's good to talk to people on the down-low and say, 'I'm looking for someone to help me out with something.'"

Building supportive relationships isn't just important in terms of professional development, but also for personal wellbeing:

"You need to have that ability to be vulnerable. You can be vulnerable to your line manager but you can't necessarily open up if you're really struggling. You might not want to do that. I think it's really useful having a group of people who I can go to and talk about the issues that I'm dealing with. You've got that opportunity to share and talk a bit more. If you're an aspiring leader, you can tap into that a little bit by getting a mentor. Somebody to talk to about it so you can see what it's like behind the fence, I suppose. It just gives you that realisation of what it's really like because it's not all glamour, is it?"

The importance of having a support network, whether inside or beyond your school, is something that was stressed by all the leaders I interviewed.

✳ Sometimes working harder and harder isn't the answer

If you are feeling like an imposter or that you have to prove yourself, it can be very easy to get into a cycle of working harder and harder, later and later, just to get that one final thing done and prove your worthiness. Ben recounted a light-bulb moment he had about this approach:

"I just remember on a Sunday feeling like, 'Oh no, I've got to do more work!' but not doing it and automatically feeling guilty. My boss, the head, told me

that was mental. She said I was intellectually self-harming by not doing more work but thinking that I needed to. So now I realise that when you've walked out of the school door, you're no longer the leader. You need to go home. You need to relax and have quiet time and recharge because at 7 a.m. the next day you need to be ready in a way that is actually going to benefit people."

Ben has also realised the value of making time for life outside of work and has improved his own mental and physical health since finding the time to commit to the high-intensity fitness regimen CrossFit:

"I needed to make the choice to get healthy. It was New Year's Eve, I was in Victoria Park in London with my mate, eating a pot noodle, and I realised, 'You need to sort your life out.' I was perennially tired, and felt like I couldn't do any exercise because I'd come home from work and be so tired. But actually I was like, 'I'm tired because I'm not doing anything.' I think I suddenly realised, 'I've got to do this.'"

✳ Your view is not the only one

As a senior leader you may feel passionately about a particular initiative, but not everybody in your school community will think in the same way as you. I've learnt this the hard way. Ben always tries to put the needs of the students at the centre of decision making, and informs his views with reading and research:

"We've all been in meetings with one person who really wants to force their argument through. Does it make an improvement in practice? I don't know. Does it improve the quality of teaching and the education of the students? Probably not. Is someone pushing an agenda? Most likely."

Ben explained his own thought processes as a leader. He tries to always consider other people's points of view, take a measured approach to meetings and debate and remain wary of authoritative behaviours:

"Whenever I'm thinking of an issue or something I'm trying to put in place, I will always automatically think of the counterarguments. So I can pre-empt them and address them. I think my law degree is partly to blame for that as well. Shouting an argument down doesn't mean you're right. Your voice might be the loudest but it does not mean you are right, and I just find that approach really frustrating."

The power of the quieter voices is a theme we will return to in the next chapter when we meet Lila.

Parting words

At the end of our interview, Ben had specific advice for anyone who is unsure whether they are ready to take on their next challenge or feels that they are not yet experienced enough or are new to post and worried that they might get "found out":

"If you are good and you can do it, then just do it. Your race, your age, your sexuality, your gender, or whatever has bugger all to do with it at the end of the day. If you can do it, then do it now. Don't worry if your face doesn't fit. Do you want to be in an organisation where your face needs to fit? If you get knocked back, that doesn't mean that you can't do it. Just go again. If I didn't take this opportunity and I was still doing my head of department job now, I feel like I would be sat there thinking, 'I could have done that. I'm sure I could have.' The worst thing would be to sit there saying, 'I could have done it better than that person.' Which is a bit cocky, but you never know, do you?"

PART II
HUMANITY

Humanity

As leaders, it can sometimes feel as if we are seen as our roles first and people second. However, it's important not to forget our humanity. We each come with our own personalities and personal values – and if we are to be able to live authentically, and look ourselves in the mirror, then these must shape our approach to leadership and our interactions with staff, students and the wider communities we serve. The question is, how can we be effective leaders without sacrificing who we are?

CHAPTER 3

I am an introvert – Lila's story

"I'm small, I'm Indian, I'm not loud. We all have an image of what a leader should be and that image is typically a suited white man. It's a very powerful image and hard to shift."

You

❋ Do you hate making whole-staff announcements?

❋ In meetings, do you prefer to listen to the points made and process what is being said rather than feel the need to convince everybody of your opinion?

❋ Are you happy to develop other people rather than take the credit for everything?

❋ Are you confident in your abilities but don't feel the need to self-publicise?

❋ Have you ever been told that you need to speak up and be more vocal and confident in meetings or with your colleagues?

❋ Are you just as comfortable alone as you are with other people? Sometimes more so?

❋ Are you happy working in a team and with others but sometimes need to work alone to really concentrate and process?

❋ If you answered yes to any of these questions then you may identify as an introvert. At the very least, you may have a quieter leadership style and be happiest out of the spotlight.

There is a perception that leaders need to be extroverted, outgoing and charismatic. Many people may feel that these qualities are synonymous or interchangeable. They believe that leaders need to be the brightest light in the room that all are drawn to. This isn't necessarily the case. There are valuable traits that introverts bring to leadership, and there are effective leaders who would be identified as such. However, people don't expect introverts to make good leaders.

Me

I identify as an introvert, but for some people this has negative connotations and they'd rather not be known as such. To some, introversion is the same as shyness. It's not so for me. I'm confident when I know about a topic and I find it easy to interact and connect with people. My introversion is about how I recharge and get my energy. Some people need others around them in order to feel energised but I'm the opposite. I enjoy interacting with people but I also need long stretches of time alone and I tend to prefer being in small group or one-to-one interactions over socialising or working in large groups.

The seeds for this chapter were planted when I was an assistant head teacher and I was called into my boss' office. "Iesha," he said, "have a seat." I took the one opposite him at the huge conference table that dominated the office. So far, so normal; we met like this on a weekly basis. But next he said something which really had an impact on me. "Iesha, I don't feel like this year has been a very successful year for you, compared to last year." He went on to outline why.

I sat and listened quietly but inside, I have to be honest, I was livid. I left the meeting calmly, but internally seething. I was angry. Extremely angry. This was because, in my view, I'd actually had a more successful year than the previous one. My work had had a bigger and wider impact due to who I'd worked with and projects that I'd initiated, or so I thought. However, to outside observers it seemed that I'd had a much lower profile compared to the preceding year. Once my rage had subsided and I really thought about how I was coming across, I realised that, deep down, I couldn't be that surprised by my boss' comment.

In the year that he considered to be highly successful, I'd been extremely visible. I'd led on a staff consultation related to the school improvement plan and had led lots of middle leader meetings. This year, the one perceived to be less successful, I'd been much more behind the scenes. Much more of my work had been done in small meetings or individual coaching sessions, deliberately so, because I wanted to empower other staff and develop their leadership capacity independently of me. I felt like there had been more evidence of sustained change as a result of my work and that the impact on others would last beyond my time working with them. To me that felt much more successful, but as a result there were fewer demonstrable initiatives, so I couldn't visibly take the credit for anything.

Despite disagreeing with him at the time, I can now see that my boss did me a favour. After that meeting, I realised that my style as an introvert will occasionally mean that the perception of me is that I'm not effective even if the reality is different. Knowing this could empower me to do something about it. My boss was supportive and we subsequently found projects that made use of my skillset while giving me a platform to be more visible. That experience taught me that in our working lives, whether we like it or not, perception is very important, as the perception of you becomes other people's reality.

For introverts, perception can be the enemy. There is the perception that we are shy. The perception that we are less effective compared to people who are happier being in the limelight or trumpeting their achievements. That meeting started a journey which made me consider how I am perceived and how I can use my generally introverted traits as strengths. I first shared my ideas about being an introverted leader publicly during a talk at a major education conference. The reception from the audience of school leaders, and the subsequent interactions I had, made me realise that I had to write about this topic as it resonates with many people. I hope that if you are reading this an introverted school leader it will help you to see your strengths and help you avoid some of the mistakes that I made which caused others to question my worth and effectiveness.

Lila

Lila is the principal of an academy in the east Midlands. Her school is oversubscribed and well thought of in the area. She identifies as an introvert even though she's "not sure that it's a positive label". Lila has been teaching English for over thirty years. She loves teaching Shakespeare because of the "richness of language and the enduring, universal themes". This might be a surprise to her own childhood teachers because she came to the UK from Uganda as a refugee aged 9, speaking very little English. Growing up, Lila's family did not have many books – money was tight due to their refugee status and this was a luxury they could ill afford – but her own home now is lined with shelves of them. One title I noticed when visiting was *Quiet*. In it, Susan Cain says of introverts, "in leadership positions they execute with quiet competence" and this a theme that recurred throughout my interview with Lila.[1]

Lila's story shows that, if you find the right environment and a cause you really believe in, your skills as an introverted leader can be put to good use and have real benefit for the community you serve. Lila has worked in a number of schools but she chose to lead her current school, where she taught for over a decade before becoming principal, because many of the students are from families who fled Uganda at the time that hers did. "I just knew I wanted a school where I felt a connection with the students and the community," she says.

Lila is no stranger to self-doubt. She didn't actively pursue leadership earlier on in her life, feeling that she didn't quite measure up to the mould:

> "I didn't ever think I was good enough to be a principal. I still have moments of doubt. I went to about five different primary schools between the ages of 9 and 10 and then I went to a very liberal inner-city secondary school which wasn't very academic at all. There was no uniform. We were on first-name terms with our teachers. It was very interdisciplinary subject wise. I didn't study history and geography because we did some sort of project work, which I enjoyed and obviously engaged with, but looking back it's given me huge gaps in my knowledge. I've always felt that I don't know enough. I've waited for promotion to happen, rather than chasing it. You have to keep being quietly competent. Posts have come up, people have said, 'You should go for it' or, 'You should apply' or I've been sort of given posts covertly. I guess I've always waited to be recognised rather than put myself forward. I would urge other people to go for it but that's never been my style."

---

1 Susan Cain, *Quiet: The Power of Introverts in a World That Can't Stop Talking* (London: Penguin, 2013), p. 13.

When I asked Lila why she thought this was, she said:

> "I'm small, I'm Indian, I'm not loud. We all have an image of what a leader should be and that image is typically a suited white man. It's a very powerful image and hard to shift. Not only in our heads but in the heads of others."

Lila traces being underestimated by others back to her own school days:

> "It was the 1970s and I was part of a new tranche of migration in Coventry. I think now national statistics show Indian students succeed, so teachers typically have a certain view of them – but at that time it certainly wasn't expected of me, so there was surprise when I got my O level results.[2] Teachers were astounded because I got As. This has continued in the professional context, but I feel like now it is to do with my size, to do with my ethnicity, to do with my gender. These are the reasons people are surprised by me. They don't expect competence and flair and leadership in that package."

Lila recalled the time she expressed an interest in applying for a senior leadership position at a previous school:

> "I didn't feel that people got me there, so I had to work really hard to show my worth. It was a girls' school, more middle class than any other I'd worked in. The staff weren't as open as I've found people in my current school, but then it was just my sheer competence that won them over. Not in a showy way; in a really unconfident way, actually. It tested me. I definitely wasn't seen as a senior leader, I remember once there was a senior leader position advertised and there was a briefing for teachers who were interested. I was

---

2   According to the data, students with Indian heritage do outperform white British students at GCSE in maths and English. Department for Education, Revised GCSE and Equivalent Results in England: 2016 to 2017. Ref: SFR01/2018 [statistical first release] (25 January 2018). Available at: https://www.gov.uk/government/statistics/revised-gcse-and-equivalent-results-in-england-2016-to-2017.

head of English at the time and I went along. The vice principal asked, 'Why are you here?' I said, 'Oh, I thought I'd find out about the post,' and she replied, 'Really?' in a very bemused way. I could tell she was thinking, 'Why is she here?' That's when I knew I had to leave that school, I just knew it wasn't where I needed to be."

As well as not being seen as a leader by others, Lila struggled to consider herself as having influence – part of which she attributes to her natural introversion, and to perceptions of gender in the culture in which she grew up:

"I have struggled to make friends throughout my life. I am introverted. I'm part of a large family, there are five children: four girls and a boy. In Indian families, boys are absolutely, unapologetically at a premium. The whole family wealth and security resides in the son. So that's important in why, I suppose, I didn't feel that I was going to be a leader. In my teenage years, my weekends were spent going to weddings or receiving people who were considering proposals for my older sisters, because I was the youngest. Our whole lives were consumed by matchmaking and weddings and it was like Sense and Sensibility! *I used to take my book along and read at weddings. There are videos of me at weddings reading a book, and I really stand out because obviously I'm the only person doing it. Being clever makes you a little bit lonely as a child, although you don't realise it at the time because you think everybody is the same as you. I've always had very different interests from my cousins but also couldn't really embrace the interests of the wider community, so there's that sense of loneliness and isolation."*

Lila feels that her ability to carefully observe people and exist on the edges is an asset as a head, especially when coupled with her sense of social justice:

"I am introverted. I'm much better on my own and reading but this searing sense of idealism and wanting to do well by the world thrusts you into movements like education so you are able to play your part and be part of

the life of others, I suppose. As a principal, introversion helps you identify with the vulnerable students. You see things more. If you get your school right for the most vulnerable, then it's probably right for everybody else. You also observe more, so you notice the dynamics in your teams and because you are watching and listening and waiting, because you're not diving in there and taking up all the air space, people actually reveal themselves in all sorts of ways. That's helped with my confidence and leadership because the loudest people, you realise, aren't always doing the best work, whereas at first you think they are."

Lila discovered earlier in her career that quiet leaders can find their own way to have impact, away from the spotlight, by building relationships and paying attention to detail:

"When I became a pastoral leader, with oversight of over 400 students, I took over from this massive guy who had completely failed at the role. He could do the booming scary bit with pupils but there was no follow-through. When I came along, I thought, 'How am I going to win the confidence of these pupils and the teachers?' I surprised myself because I did it really well, even with the most challenging kids. It was just sheer persistence, listening, following through on absolutely everything and being really, really consistent. Explaining to heightened parents, heightened students, why they couldn't do certain things. Saying the word 'no', but not in a way that destroyed them. I was able to connect with the most challenging kids because I treated them as human beings and treated their families that way too. I managed to win them over. I always collected the kids for detention, I noticed none of the other pastoral leaders did. Teachers had the confidence to refer students to me."

What can we learn from Lila's story?

✳ We can teach our students that it's okay to be quiet

Lila reflected that generally schools are very sociable places where extroversion is implicitly prized and as educators we should question that:

> "You know what? We as teachers compound it over time. We may have a quiet student and when we write reports and at parents' evenings we always say, 'She needs to contribute more to lessons.' But you know what? Maybe she doesn't. Maybe her contribution is all in her head and not everybody can or needs to vocalise, but society is built around loud voices."

✳ Build a team around you of different types of people

It's easy to be drawn to people who are like us. Lila explained how she had purposefully constructed a leadership team who complemented her skills but were different:

> "When we appointed my deputy we had another credible candidate but they were really like me. I think you've got to surround yourself with different people and that works conversely as well. The really extrovert and loud people need a few introverts on their team. As long as you share a moral purpose, you need a wide range of styles."

I remember once having a similar conversation with my head teacher during a line management meeting. He was very clear that he had chosen each of the people on the SLT for our skill and moral purpose but also because we each had different skillsets and approaches that didn't come naturally to him. When I probed further, he was clear that we were different from him and from each other and he had chosen us deliberately to create a strong multi-faceted team.

✳ Quiet leaders can be strong and make tough decisions

Lila is a successful principal and has shown that she is able to make tough decisions, ones that predecessors have avoided. If you are quiet or introverted you can still be a strong leader:

> *"When I became a principal, there was this one maths leader. We were the first Asian teachers in the school, we had started together, there was a bit of a bond there, a personal relationship. We had our children at the same time and had helped each other through divorce and bereavement, but I had always been alarmed at her lack of commitment to the role. Maths is a high-achieving subject in our school because our families are really well-disposed to maths and engage tutors and so on, but there was an issue in terms of low-ability and disadvantaged students not doing well. Also this leader was not leading the faculty very well, there were elements of bullying in her style. Others had known about it in the past but nothing had ever been done. I felt that I ought to act but because she was a friend of mine it really muddied the waters. I found it so hard. I felt wretched and knotted with guilt. I had to put her on a plan. I instituted capability proceedings. I had union involvement. It became really, really messy. Half of me just wanted to say, 'Oh no, let's bury it.' Ultimately our friendship had to go. It was really, really heavy and so sapping personally, but the right thing to do. If it's the right thing to do you've got to do it. And you can't hide behind any excuse."*

✳ Find your supporters and leave when you and your skills are not valued

It can be easy to stay in a situation feeling that you are wrong and need to change. Sometimes you may do. Other times, the organisation is not the right fit for you and your skills will be more valued elsewhere. I have previously wasted so much time trying to mould myself into a style of leader that wasn't really me, only to move to another workplace and find that those same skills that were previously overlooked are highly prized. Lila has some clear advice here:

"I am fundamentally optimistic. There are always people out there who are willing to help. Have the confidence to know that people somewhere will get you and will see your worth, but if you're in a place where they don't, you have to move. If I'd stayed at my other school, I'd never have been a principal, so you've got to find places that will allow you to flourish. I have been fortunate in my career that people have noticed me even though I haven't been the most vocal in meetings. I think it's not about how much you say, it's what you say. I like to read. I like to really get a handle on something and then make my contribution and I hope it will be a really thoughtful, insightful one. You have to have people around you who will wait for that and who will recognise it when you do contribute. I've been fortunate with our executive head, and with the principal before me."

To add to Lila's point about meetings, if speaking up is not your thing, following up and adding your comments via email can be a good workaround. It lets colleagues know that you are engaged but allows you to contribute on your own terms.

✳ Put yourself in somebody else's shoes

Not wanting to be the centre of attention can make you very observant and aware of others. Lila outlined how this can help in her decision-making process:

"It makes me really think through every change that I make. I can really place myself in that position and ask myself how will it feel for a student, how will it feel for a middle leader, how will it feel for a teacher if we do this? And how would I feel? That really guides my mission. It doesn't stop me doing tough things but it makes me do so in a way that will be the least detrimental in terms of workload and morale."

When introducing a new tracking system, which was needed for improvement but could have had workload implications for staff, Lila had a discussion with the SLT member leading on the area:

"I said, 'You show me on my laptop. I'm going to time you, and if it takes more than fifteen minutes, we're not sending the email out.' Every time there's an adaptation, my rule is, 'Not more than fifteen minutes', and demonstrate it to me first before it goes out to middle leaders."

✳ Plan and prepare for public speaking opportunities

Speaking in public can cause many naturally quiet or introverted leaders to be nervous. It needn't be this way:

"For my first assembly, I carefully structured the message that I wanted to give about the use of praise as well as sanctions. I got such good feedback after every assembly and that made me feel really confident because I hadn't done assemblies prior to that role."

My experiences have been similar to Lila's. I always planned my assemblies in the same way that I did my lessons. Public speaking wasn't something that came naturally to me and I hadn't really had to do many assemblies until I became an assistant head. I always chose a topic that I was passionate about and tailored it specifically to the year group. With time, I got better and less nervous. I often got staff and students coming up to me to comment on assemblies that I'd given. I was surprised one day when a colleague who I didn't know very well came to tell me that her Year 7 class had told her that they always enjoyed my assemblies. She had come to ask for tips about how to prepare one. I was pleasantly surprised to learn that I was making an impression in an area that I initially didn't feel particularly confident in. Again, it's all a question of other people's perceptions.

✳ Having formal support structures can help build confidence

Lila reflected that she was confident in her abilities as a leader now, but initially she was less secure, so having the support of her MAT was useful earlier on.

"Being part of a MAT is really helpful, as is having an executive head. I don't know if I would have been a principal otherwise. You're working with others and ultimately you're all aligned and have loyalty to the trust, so that makes you less isolated. I think MATs and CEOs will enable more introverted people to rise to headship because you know that you've always got that other layer there that you can call on."

For Lila it was her MAT, for you it could be your federation or others in your local authority or local teaching school alliance.

Parting words

If you have leadership skills but are reluctant to put yourself forward, Lila has a message about what she calls servant leadership that can help by making the decision to lead more about your impact on others:[3]

"For me, servant leadership is where your commitment, your dedication, your work, arises from the needs of others. So you are serving the needs of the parents and the students and you are there as a leader, but you are serving a greater purpose."

Lila's final words echoed a sentiment expressed by Ben in Chapter 2, you never really find out if you can do a job until you are actually in post:

"It is just taking that step. You can't really prepare for being a head teacher other than by doing it, but that's the same in every role. You have to do the role. You have to throw yourself in. That's the whole of life though, isn't it?"

---

3 Cheryl Williamson, Servant Leadership: How to Put Your People Before Yourself, *Forbes* (19 July 2017). Available at: https://www.forbes.com/sites/forbescoachescouncil/2017/07/19/servant-leadership-how-to-put-your-people-before-yourself/#55e6b85066bc.

CHAPTER 4

I'll shoulder the consequences of speaking out – Tait's story

*"I don't want people to think like me.
I just want them to think."*

You

* Do you have a strong social conscience?

* Maybe you believe that certain things in society need to be changed and that education is part of the solution.

* Maybe you look around your local community and think that your school can be a place that actively challenges the expectations of the young people you serve, and their families.

* Whatever your precise situation, you feel strongly and you care, but this is not ego driven.

* Your personal situation may be fine. You are in leadership and respected but you want to improve the situation for your whole school community.

* Now that you are in senior leadership, or will be soon, you feel you are in a position to change things.

* But you are scared. There doesn't seem to be a general appetite for change.

* So how outspoken can you be?

* Sometimes colleagues make noises that support you behind closed doors but in public they are nowhere to be seen. Should you give up?

* Should you keep quiet?

* Should you just support the status quo?

* How can you act in a way that fits your beliefs, while using your position to try to extend the access and opportunities that you currently enjoy to members of your school community who don't share these advantages?

If, like me, you have wrestled with questions like these, then read on. I can't promise all the answers but I can show you that you are not alone. I hope you will take something away from Tait's story. I certainly learnt a lot from talking to him.

Me

Throughout my career I have struggled with knowing how much I can say about topics that I feel very strongly about but which could be considered controversial. For me, these topics relate to social class, school hierarchies – and especially managers treating staff well – and, occasionally, race. I'm generally very open in expressing my views with colleagues, but the real consideration for me is knowing what I can say outside of private meetings and in the public sphere, whether that's with the wider staff or beyond my school community. I have sometimes worried about what would happen if my views were interpreted as being fundamentally opposed to the school's or to wider government initiatives. I don't think I'm the only person in school leadership who has felt this way.

The Guardian has an ongoing column called "The Secret Teacher" where teachers, and school leaders, write anonymously about topics that matter to them.[1] They write anonymously because they fear repercussions. Head teachers in my professional network have felt compelled to blog anonymously because they didn't feel able to fully express how they felt about government policies and issues that affected the work of their schools under their own professional identities.[2]

I started writing publicly in a personal blog about my teaching life in 2013, during my second head of maths role. I found it a useful place to reflect on and process what I believed professionally. I continued the blog into my first senior leadership role, a secondment as an assistant head. I was careful not to name my school, colleagues or students and my reflections were personal. It detailed my mistakes and my learning, my musings and questions as a middle and then senior leader, as well as wider thoughts on the education system and on society in general. Occasionally, I would stray into more political or contentious territory, but my school knew me well and it wasn't a problem.

---

1 See, for example, The Secret Teacher, Secret Teacher: I Protect and Nurture My Staff Like a Doting Parent, *The Guardian* (4 June 2016). Available at: https://www.theguardian.com/teacher-network/2016/jun/04/secret-teacher-protect-nurture-staff-parent-senior-leadership-team.
2 One leader I know used to maintain an anonymous blog but it became defunct when their identity was revealed. The about page simply says, "I probably shouldn't blog. But I do". See https://chocotzarht.wordpress.com/about/.

Then I got a new job in a new school and, as I mentioned in the introduction, I suddenly stopped writing. To reiterate, nobody ever said anything to me about it. Any censorship was self-imposed and entirely to do with my own self-perception, but in any case I suddenly felt unable to publicly express myself. I was acutely aware of my position as an SLT member, representing a new school where people didn't know me well yet. I felt like I couldn't express any opinion that might be remotely misconstrued and it meant that my writing output dropped to virtually nothing because I didn't want to be stuck writing bland posts that didn't fully reflect what I thought.

Tait

I was first introduced to Tait's work about a year after I started my own blog. He had just written *Never Mind the Inspectors: Here's Punk Learning*, which one review described as "a no nonsense, in your face and cut the crap book" and one of my colleagues had been excitedly sharing many of the ideas in it and had based a staff training session around it.[3] Tait is a senior leader and proud teacher of science in a comprehensive secondary school in West Yorkshire. He is passionate about teaching and learning and sees pedagogy as a means to empower students. Tait grew up in a quiet village in Northamptonshire but was awoken to inequality in society by the punk music that he listened to while at sixth form and via the visible inequality he saw while at university in a big city.

Senior leaders are in the position to create a climate that really challenges the norms of society and the communities that they are part of, but this can be a scary prospect. Although you are in a position of authority, you still need to enforce the rules of the school as well as fulfilling statutory duties. It is much easier to be bland, vanilla, safe and neutral because of potential ramifications for yourself or the school than it is to fly the flag for what you really believe in. It can be especially difficult if you stand out in some obvious way as a leader in your school

---

3 Tait Coles, *Never Mind the Inspectors: Here's Punk Learning* (Carmarthen: Independent Thinking Press, 2014). For the review see John Dabell, Punk Learning, *Teacher Toolkit* [blog] (12 March 2017). Available at: https://www.teachertoolkit.co.uk/2017/03/12/punk-learning/.

or local context and so don't want to draw further attention to yourself. Many of us want to believe that we stand up for what we believe in, but what does that mean in practice? Perhaps most of us only speak out about societal issues if they directly affect us or when it's convenient and there is nothing for us to lose. This is understandable. We are scared. We don't want to be targets but, ultimately, saying and doing nothing eats away at us.

If you became a school leader to make a difference and you are actively interested in changing and improving an unequal and unfair society, Tait's story will inspire you. He explains how he has used his specific role as a deputy head teacher in charge of teaching and learning to act on his beliefs that "the education system should inspire and mobilise – rather than mould – students into understanding the relationship between knowledge and power". This is a process that he hopes will lead to "self-emancipation for many of our students who are currently part of a deliberately unequal system".

I wanted to interview Tait as somebody who I perceive to be consistently true to his beliefs when both speaking and writing publicly, but also as somebody whose beliefs underpin everything that he has done as a leader within his school community. Tait has stuck to his core beliefs in practice even when these have made people uncomfortable. Arguably it would be easier for him, as a white middle-class man who is personally unaffected by some of the issues he speaks out about, to maintain the status quo.

Tait has publicly opposed Prevent, a controversial government initiative which Lord Carlile – who led the review into it at the request of the then home secretary, Theresa May – described as, "a template for challenging the extremist ideas and terrorist actions which seek to undermine the rule of law and fundamental British political values and institutions".[4] Schools have been cited as key institutions in

---

4   Quoted in Home Office and the Rt Hon Theresa May MP, New Prevent Strategy Launched [press release] (7 June 2011). Available at: https://www.gov.uk/government/news/new-prevent-strategy-launched. The report in question is Alex Carlile, *Report to the Home Secretary of Independent Oversight of Prevent Review and Strategy* (London: Home Office, 2011). Available at: https://assets.publishing.service.gov.uk/government/uploads/system/uploads/attachment_data/file/97977/lord-carlile-report.pdf.

the implementation of Prevent.[5] Tait has expressed opposition because he feels the Prevent strategy, especially in its original form, disproportionately affects young people in the types of community that his school serves. Tait's approach has brought some potentially career-ending negative professional consequences, but he still feels he has done what is right according to his own values. I admire that bravery and strive to be that sort of person and professional too.

Tait started his working life as a scientist but something about his work for a large soft drinks manufacturer left him feeling hollow:

> "I worked in a lab for a well-known cola brand, testing all the drinks to make sure they were within the parameters of what the company wanted. It was good money but after a while I just went home thinking, 'I haven't really achieved anything. Drinking fizzy drinks is leading to a massive obesity crisis across the world.' There was no sense of 'I'm making a difference here.'"

Tait's work felt a long way from the idealism of his youth when he was first introduced to punk music and got a sense of the inequalities around him:

> "In the sixth form I got into politics through music. I listened to bands that talked about people and ideas I'd never heard of. Paul Weller was always talking about quotes from George Orwell's 1984. Joe Strummer from The Clash would be talking about the Spanish Civil War. It opened up a different way of thinking, made me start to realise, 'The world's not really fair, is it? The country's not really fair.'"

Tait's awareness of inequality increased when he went to university and he experienced a different world to the one he had grown up in:

---

5   Home Office, *Prevent Review: Summary of Responses to the Consultation* (June 2011). Available at: https://assets.publishing.service.gov.uk/government/uploads/system/uploads/attachment_data/file/97978/prevent-summary-consultation.pdf, p. 11.

"I grew up in a little village just outside Northampton and I wasn't really exposed to visible inequality, but I went up to university in Leeds and I saw it more and started to think in really simple terms. 'Oh, you shouldn't have people on the streets with no money, with nowhere to live, and next door to them is a five-star hotel where people spend £250 a night for a room.'"

Tait graduated and worked as a scientist for a while, in his well-paying but increasingly morally unsatisfying job at the drinks company. Then he decided it was time for a career change that would allow him to tackle some of the issues he had felt strongly about in his youth:

"It's probably what got me into the classroom. You've got an hour with thirty kids. You can make a difference. Right from early doors of teaching, I was, and still am, proud to be a teacher. You have a responsibility. School is not just teaching kids facts, it's teaching them about the world. If you are in charge of teaching and learning you're trying to inspire teachers to educate kids. I think education isn't just about exam results, retention of knowledge, remembering stuff. It's a lot more than that. If you think about big private schools, like Wellington, they do it right.[6] They are educators. They teach kids who do well in exams but they also educate their students about everything else in the world and I think that's missing in a lot of schools. Some people just see themselves as teachers rather than educators. For a lot of kids, the teachers and the head teacher are the only people with authority who they might see and interact with. So I think it's important that they see an authority figure who is open to expressing their views."

Earlier in his teaching career, Tait spent a year as a subject adviser for his borough and worked with several local schools. What he saw, read and researched during that time shaped his current views about teaching and learning and how education should impact society as well as individual students:

---

6 Wellington College is a co-educational, independent day and boarding school in Berkshire, England. See https://www.wellingtoncollege.org.uk/.

"The learning vision that we have in our school is based on critical pedagogy.[7] It's based on the students having the desire and knowledge to become powerful, making our students become empowered. Critical pedagogy means that students have a social conscience and are aware of their own place in society, and are aware of how society influences them and how they influence society. That, importantly, they have the skills and the desire to make a difference. Not only to themselves, 'I need to achieve. I need to hit my target grade. Don't worry about anyone else.' That's very much about individualism, about one person succeeding. Critical pedagogy is all about a society achieving. Making it better for yourself and making it better for other people."

After his time as a borough adviser and then head of science, Tait became an AST, helping other teachers to improve their practice. When Tait realised that he wanted to become an SLT member, there was one specific role that he felt would allow him to do work that really mattered to him across the school:

"Behaviour, data, timetabling and special educational needs coordinator (SENCO) are all really important roles on an SLT but for me it was always about teaching and learning, about pedagogy, about training staff. All that I was interested in ties in with that. I don't think people in other roles on the SLT possibly could or would want to talk about equality and injustice and society in their role, but I think if you're in charge of teaching and learning then you're in charge of educating young people. That's why I wanted to become assistant head, deputy head, vice principal or whatever of teaching and learning. It's the perfect position, in my mind."

---

7   Critical Pedagogy is most associated with Brazilian activist and educator Paulo Freire and "is concerned with transforming relations of power which are oppressive and which lead to the oppression of people. It tries to humanize and empower learners". Quoted in Mohammad Aliakbari and Elham Faraji, Basic Principles of Critical Pedagogy, *International Proceedings of Economics Development and Research* 17 (2011): 77–85 at 77. Available at: http://www.ipedr.com/vol17/14-CHHSS%202011-H00057.pdf.

Tait used his position on the SLT to start difficult conversations with the teaching staff about topics that felt taboo and to galvanise staff to address the realities of life for many of the students that they taught:

"The school I'm working at currently has a high proportion of working-class, Pakistani, Muslim students. It's a comprehensive, non-faith school and we serve the demographic of kids who live in the area. It's a brilliant school. The kids are wonderful. But you'd see and hear teachers, when they were describing who some students were, they would whisper the word 'Muslim' – almost like they were frightened to talk about that.[8] So the SLT created opportunities in training sessions where staff could talk, in departments, about the contexts of the students. There were a lot of assumptions, a lot of ill-informed ideas from people who've been in that school for ten, fifteen years but didn't know about the contexts of the students. The class of our students, the ethnicity and the religion of our students.

"White members of staff and non-Muslim members of staff were really worried about saying something that might offend Muslim staff. In fact, some Muslim staff felt uncomfortable about discussing ethnicity and religion because they didn't want to be seen as banging on about something that people wouldn't be interested in. We set up quite a few sessions to allow staff the opportunity to feel confident about talking about the contexts of the students. I felt that was really important, in the same way that if you work in a white working-class school you'd talk about the context.

"I used to start off a lot of our staff meetings reeling off statistics about the inequality facing people in Bradford and about the proportion of

---

8   Survey data supports Tait's point that teachers are uncomfortable talking about contentious issues; 32% of male staff and 27% of female staff reported that they didn't think staff were comfortable talking about race or sexism. Rachael Pells, Black and Ethnic Minority Teachers Face 'Invisible Glass Ceiling' in Schools, Report Warns, *The Independent* (14 April 2017). Available at: https://www.independent. co.uk/news/education/education-news/black-asian-ethnic-minority-teachers-invisible-glass-ceiling-racism-schools-report-runnymeade-nut-a7682026.html.

unemployment in Bradford. I wanted to get the point across to teachers that it's not just about the grades. That actually, if a kid from our school leaves with good grades, they've got a lesser chance of securing a university place than someone else, which isn't fair.[9] It's kind of over to us. What are we going to do about it? To make teachers aware of it. There's no quick fix but it's something that we always need to bear in mind."

Tait routinely discusses uncomfortable topics in his school community and is used to writing publicly about controversial topics. He is not one to shy away from sharing his views. He once wrote an article in a national newspaper criticising Teach First, the charity that places high-achieving graduates in schools in low-income communities across the UK for a two-year commitment, suggesting that it was based on a mistaken premise and was "narcissistic".[10] However, one day he wrote a blog post which had serious implications for his career and livelihood:

"I wrote a personal blog post that fundamentally disagreed with Prevent, a major government strategy aimed at preventing radicalisation and terrorism. It discussed the criticisms of the strategy based upon lots of evidence, lots of research, but also with some ideas about what we could do as a teaching profession and as individual teachers. There was a complaint against me. I never saw the specifics but I was under investigation of being associated with government 'prescribed groups', like terrorist groups.

---

9   In a synthesis of research, Shaw et al. report that "university applications and admissions data suggests that the proportion of students from minority ethnic groups who receive an offer of a pace [sic] at Russell Group Universities is lower than would be expected given prior academic performance. The authors argue that this is especially the case for Bangladeshi, Pakistani and Black students." Shaw et al., *Ethnicity, Gender and Social Mobility* (London: Social Mobility Commission, 2016). Available at: https://assets.publishing.service.gov.uk/government/uploads/system/uploads/attachment_data/file/579988/Ethnicity_gender_and_social_mobility.pdf, pp. 40–41.

10   Tait Coles, Critical Pedagogy: Schools Must Equip Students to Challenge the Status Quo, *The Guardian* (25 February 2014). Available at: https://www.theguardian.com/teacher-network/teacher-blog/2014/feb/25/critical-pedagogy-schools-students-challenge.

"The complaint said I wasn't teaching or agreeing with fundamental British values. I had to be interviewed to prove that I was. So I had to talk about democracy and individual liberty and the rule of law. It was all minuted to say that I wasn't part of any terrorist groups. There was lots of fear for me, and I didn't want to bring the school into disrepute. I didn't want to put any undue pressure on the kids. Then it led to frustration, annoyance, a little bit of anger. After a while a small part of me thought, 'Well I must be doing something right if people are complaining.' I was very professional but it upset me. I still think about it quite a bit. Perhaps it stopped me from writing more. It's perhaps made me more aware of my position as a leader. The topic is hot potato stuff. If you talk about the radicalisation of pupils, it's controversial."

Tait's experience made him reflect on what he writes about in the public sphere, and the reasons why school leaders may feel uncomfortable speaking out about controversial issues. But this hasn't driven him underground:

"There was a sense of having my wings clipped a little bit. But I understand the investigation. I was a member of that school. I was a leader in that school. I was a teacher in that school. But I would never write anonymously. I don't see the point. I want to put my name to what I say and write because I'm not ashamed to say it and I'm proud of what I say. I think it's right. But I'm aware that if you put your name to it, you also put your school's name, and that's a completely different kettle of fish. It's almost like self-censorship, isn't it? I think leaders, especially head teachers, don't share their views vocally as much. When I started out being a teacher, being a leader, I perhaps didn't have the armoury to choose which way I wanted to express my thoughts. Writing should be dangerous. You should write to make people think."

What can we learn from Tait's story?

✳ Don't wait for others to take the lead

Sometimes it would be much easier not to speak up about difficult issues, especially if they don't directly affect us. For example, why do you need to comment on the difference in the staff paid sick day policy for teachers versus teaching assistants if you are a teacher and it doesn't affect you? I asked Tait why he felt the need to discuss and challenge assumptions about race, religion and class. As a white, middle-class man, wouldn't it be easier for him to shut up and enjoy his position in life, leaving it to people who are actually affected? He was clear in his response:

> "I think it's important because no one else is going to do it. And I've never been a person who will stand back and say, 'Someone else will do it, I'll just back them up.' I suppose I'm just using and abusing my white privilege to be able to say stuff. There's still not enough Muslim or BAME leaders in our town in secondary and primary. It doesn't fit the demographic of the people who live here and that's something that we need to address."

Tait uses his position as a leader and opportunities as a writer to address and speak out about what he thinks are injustices. I learnt from him that if we have a platform we should use it intelligently rather than being bland and safe.

✳ Be informed and clear about your view

There are situations in meetings when you can be silenced or feel coerced into changing an opinion that you know to be right and well-informed because it is unpopular or has annoyed somebody influential in the room. Tait reflected with regret on times when he did this earlier in his career:

> "It upsets me to think of times when I didn't defend my views and stick to my guns. I've learnt through being a leader and a teacher that if you are

informed about your decision and you're informed about your ideas, you should stick with them."

Knowing ahead of time what you think and why, possibly even having some notes, can help in these situations when issues are very important to you. The importance of being informed and well-prepared was also echoed by other leaders I interviewed, including Ben in Chapter 2, Lila in Chapter 3 and Malcolm, who we'll meet in the next chapter.

✳ A temporary change can shape your ideas and give you a fresh perspective

In the early part of his career, Tait was concentrating on developing his ability to teach well. However, after he became head of science he was ready for a change that ultimately affected the course of his career. He calls this his "sabbatical":

"I always said to the kids, 'No, you're going to leave before I do', because they were so used to people just coming in for a year, six months, a term, sometimes even a week, before they would leave. My form, my Year 11 group, were leaving. So I thought, 'Right, that's the perfect time to go.' An opportunity that came up, working for Education Bradford, as it was known then. It was a conscious decision to come away from the classroom to do some reading, some writing, some listening and watching. The plan was to do that for a year and then go back into school. Which I did. I did lots of reading. Lots of understanding about pedagogy. Understanding why things worked. Understanding why things didn't work. Nothing particularly radical, nothing particularly transformational. Just understanding how a classroom works and operates. How learning can be structured. Which then helped me for my next role, which led into assistant head in a school, getting in charge of teaching and learning."

Tait's period as a borough adviser was the time that allowed him to really connect his views about education with his formative ideas about inequality and societal change, developed as a young man listening to punk music:

> "The other borough advisers and I had the privilege of going into loads of schools in Bradford, seeing some great practice and some not-so-great practice and seeing how schools worked. I started getting into ideas about critical pedagogy. I met lots of new people and allowed myself to understand and listen to other views. I can't remember who said it but, 'There's no such thing as a failing school. Schools do exactly what they should be doing.' As in, some kids do really well, some kids don't: that's what society is all about. The more I read, the more failing schools I saw, the more that fight came in. In some cases, we should be doing something drastically different to what we're doing."

Our paths in leadership aren't always a straight line, as Scarlet muses in Chapter 9. Breaks from teaching, changes in role or school, these experiences can all help to shape who you are and what you believe. For Tait, the shift came from his year as a borough adviser. Karen, who we'll meet in Chapter 6, and Lila also mentioned similar periods in their careers that helped them to shape their views about their practice and educational philosophy before they eventually became heads.

✳ Change isn't always about fighting and shouting

Tait was clear that change is often about cooperation and finding common ground. Overt conflict isn't always necessary:

> "Perhaps the word challenge is wrong, people immediately imagine that you fight against it, you shout against it. Actually it's often more effective to work with your line manager, to get the best needs of the workers. It's about working with people to get the best you can from both sides. It's negotiation, isn't it?"

This is an important point. I used to think that confrontation was the way forward when I disagreed with people. Generally this just riles people. Disagreement is fine but it can be approached in a variety of ways. Ultimately you have to find a solution that means others can gain in some way too. Malcolm, who we are about to meet, has especially good advice about navigating working relationships to initiate change.

I have learnt that standing up for what you believe in can be done by various means. Sometimes the messenger affects the message that people hear. In order to challenge people, you first need to find common ground. In Tait's school, perhaps he was able to be relatively controversial about radicalisation and ethnicity because he is white – and in other ways he is like the teachers that he is talking to, so they didn't feel attacked. When people feel ashamed or defensive it's hard to get anything to actually change. When it comes to issues that are as loaded as race, religion and gender, it can be hard to even begin the conversation. But society will never change if we shy away from the discussion. I also learnt that if you want to get a message across, you don't necessarily have to be the person who delivers it. As Tait has demonstrated, getting people talking about your message is a powerful start.

* ## Take advantage of opportunities to create the world you believe in, even if your choices don't make sense to others

When I first contacted Tait to ask him to take part in this book, he was a vice principal in charge of teaching and learning. Between the time of our first emails and the time of our interview, he had taken a different opportunity in the same school which, although still on the SLT, was technically a voluntary demotion. However, he felt this fitted better into his overall beliefs:

> *"My current role is training new teachers. It was an opportunity that came up. I think those initial steps, those first years, are really important. Why would you wait until teachers are five years in to talk to them about the context of race or the context of class in education? Why not make them aware of it in*

the first year of teaching? It gives them an opportunity to discuss the issues or to ignore them or to investigate further, but at least they are in a position where they can do that themselves. I kind of wish I'd had that in my own training. Because I didn't. I had to find out for myself."

Parting words

Tait has strong views and beliefs but during our conversation it became clear that he isn't trying to convert people. Ultimately I agree with Tait that leaders should act according to their own consciences but provide opportunities for staff to think for themselves and work out their own beliefs. Tait challenges us to link our actions, beliefs and speech:

"Just after my son was born I became head of science. I suddenly looked at the students I taught in a different way. 'Would I want my children to be in that class? Would I like them to be in that school? Would I like them to be taught by that teacher?' That's a big thought process of mine. If the school's not good enough for my kids then there's got to be something we need to change. Equality is really important, but with it comes integrity. You can't talk or write about equality if your life isn't as you're trying to describe. So principles are important. I don't want people to think like me. I just want them to think. There's not many opportunities for people to discuss issues that are important."

CHAPTER 5

I'm a disrupter
– Malcolm's story

"I'm prepared to go and ask anybody the question that needs to be asked. I can do it humbly, I can do it harshly … being an SLT member … you have to ask the right questions at the right time."

You

* When others are going right do you want to go left?

* When people want to change a process do you question whether the process is even needed in the first place?

* When your colleagues are wondering how something should be done do you consider *why* it should be done?

* To you, the question is not why would you challenge this but rather why wouldn't you?

* You are curious. You disrupt others and yourself.

* You can see that there are opportunities to do things better. To solve problems that aren't being addressed. To help members of your school community who are being ignored.

* But there is a conflict. In some ways being a senior leader is about maintaining the status quo.

* How do you pick your battles?

If you've found yourself thinking about questions like these, then you could be considered a disrupter. You take the path less travelled in your organisation. Not just for the sake of it. Not just to be contrary, but because it seems the most obvious way for you to be able to help the people you've chosen to serve. You genuinely care about what is achieved rather than the minutiae of how it's done, as long as the processes don't get in the way of what is important. Your aim is to find the best possible way to benefit staff and students – even if it means changing how something is done. Even if it means a threat to your own role as it stands. It's partly why you were hired but it's also why you will have difficulties.

You don't mean to disrupt but you do. You don't mean to make others feel threatened but inevitably, unfortunately, some will be. People are comfortable with the status quo. There are systems to maintain. Egos to stroke. Apple carts not to upset. But nothing can change for the better without a little disruption. Embrace it. Read on and continue to ask questions that nobody else is asking and to take action to solve problems that others have decided are too much hassle to address.

Me

I don't think I'm especially disruptive, and I certainly don't intend to be, but in most of my school roles I have implemented major changes which others have found threatening. As a head of department, because of how I decided to deploy staff, I abolished individual performance management targets for exam classes and pushed for a single target for the whole team. This had not been done in the school before and the head wondered how I'd keep individuals accountable. Then, as an assistant head, I wanted to encourage a more open dialogue between middle and senior leaders, so for about a year I sent out a weekly series of leadership debate emails. These were a way for me to start a discussion and move away from what was sometimes criticised as a top down and autocratic management culture. Leadership debate emails had titles like "In praise of creative deviants" and "If we are adding new initiatives, what can we get rid of?" Over time I noticed highlighted printouts of these emails in classrooms and offices around the school. Middle leaders started to ask questions in person and via email that were considered and thoughtful and really challenged the established orthodoxy – which to me was part of the point, especially if it led to better outcomes for our students.

However, challenging internal practices and assumptions is not always smooth sailing. There may be people who are invested in the status quo; people you lead and your peers in leadership. Sometimes initiating change can be confusing, hard to navigate or isolating. I've often been hired as what I call the change candidate, somebody who is explicitly brought in to alter how things are done for the better. Sometimes I've been given the support and resources to do this well and other times less so.

Malcolm

I first met Malcolm when we both worked in London, at an event called HipHopEd, for educators who love the music and ethos of early underground hip hop culture and want to take innovative approaches to education and leadership.[1] These events happen a couple of times a year and are run by my friend Darren Chetty, an author, former teacher and contributor to the award-winning anthology *The Good Immigrant*.[2] Malcolm and I share a love of the nineties rapper the Notorious B.I.G. and a passion for tackling social disadvantage.

Malcolm is an assistant head teacher in his forties who grew up in London and now lives in south-west England with his family. At the time of our interview, he had been teaching for six years, having entered teaching following an earlier city career in IT. Malcolm describes himself as an educator rather than as a teacher, saying, "I think people get hung up on the term teacher because it implies qualifications and a level of status." For Malcolm, being an educator is about impacting lives and encouraging critical questions. Before becoming a qualified teacher, for many years he was involved in the supplementary school movement. Supplementary schools are community-led organisations that offer school-age children additional support with things like the curriculum and languages, as well as cultural activities.[3] At one point, while still living in London, he set up his own supplementary school to provide a broader academic and cultural education than what was on offer to children from his community in local schools at the time. He thought it was particularly important to target children from his own Afro-Caribbean background, as he'd felt a lack of opportunity while growing up. In keeping with somebody who loves to ask questions, Malcolm's favourite subjects to teach are philosophy, ethics, citizenship and personal, social, health and economic (PSHE) education,

---

1 See https://ukhiphopedblog.wordpress.com/about/.

2 Nikesh Shukla (ed.) *The Good Immigrant* (London: Unbound, 2016).

3 Incidentally, my first experience teaching maths was as a teenage volunteer at a supplementary school run on Saturday mornings by African and Caribbean parents in the area of South London where I lived at the time.

which he would describe as, "core skills that should be fundamental to our timetabled delivery in schools, yet adaptable to community and context".

I know Malcolm as a principled and thoughtful individual who is willing to ask tough questions and take difficult actions if he feels they are in the service of others and his principles. In fact, when I interviewed him he told me the story of when he worked as a department leader in the IT world before becoming a teacher. He repeatedly refused his boss' orders to sack team members to cut costs. Each time he was asked who he would sack he said, "Nobody." He exceeded the team's financial targets instead of making what he considered unnecessary staff redundancies.

After leaving the corporate world, Malcolm became a teaching assistant in a pupil referral unit (PRU) and has taken a relatively short period of time to go from there to senior leader. He feels that his career before education gave him the skills to navigate the internal politics of organisations, which is a vital skill for anybody who wants to create change from within. Malcolm describes school leadership as "easy to get wrong" and education as "liberating".

As well as being an assistant head teacher, Malcolm is also an active member of the National Education Union (NEU). In one of my assistant head roles, I'd felt that my membership of the NEU (or NUT as it was then), which actively encourages members to strike over certain issues, conflicted with my leadership role. I started my role just as the NEU was encouraging teachers to take action that was short of a strike. This meant that some of what I was expected to do as an SLT member to keep the school running undermined union colleagues, so I felt conflicted and uncomfortable. Shortly afterwards I changed unions to the Association of School and College Leaders (ASCL), which had a different approach, one that was more compatible with the role I held and the place I worked.

I wanted to know how Malcolm had managed to disrupt power structures and fixed ideas in order to create change, while actively being a part of those structures. How had he done this without undermining or alienating colleagues? This is something that I always found a difficult tightrope to walk as a senior leader, but something that any truly effective disrupter needs to learn.

Throughout our discussion, Malcolm alluded to influence in a variety of ways. His first career choice was influenced by Norman, a volunteer educator at the supplementary school he attended in the 1980s, who donated the first computer that Malcolm had ever seen:

> "My school didn't have a computer. Nobody we knew had a computer. The only place that had a computer was our education centre and that was because Norman bought it from his workplace. Once I heard that Norman was a systems analyst in IT, I said, 'I am going to be a systems analyst.' I think at 15, when I was still at supplementary school, I made a bold statement: 'I'm going work in IT then I'm going to go and be an educator.' From that point on I picked computer science in school. I did my A levels in computer science, I did my first degree in computer science. My first job was in IT."

Malcolm always had the example of others in his family who contributed to their communities in a variety of ways. A chance encounter with a former schoolmate one Christmas made Malcolm rethink his career:

> "I was becoming disillusioned with the corporate world and then I decided to do a volunteer thing one Christmas. I did this activity in North London for Crisis at Christmas and I kind of didn't know what to expect because I'd come from my nice suits and my good life.[4] I think seeing one person in particular, I won't name them, who went to my school and was a contemporary of mine when I was a kid … they didn't even recognise me but that gave me a really stark jolt. I think that was the major catalyst at about 35 when I went, 'Right, I'm just going to go do this education thing. I've lived my life, I did my thing and now I'm going to go and do something that means something.'"

---

4   Crisis is a UK homeless charity which runs special centres at Christmas. See https://www.crisis.org.uk/.

Malcolm has always had a social conscience due to the circumstances in which he had grown up, but the trappings of a life that was materially successful had made him forget about disadvantage:

> *"My mum became a teacher when she was 35, her family have always been into public service. My gran was a nurse, her sister was a nurse. Prior to that, my great grandfather was a local councillor, so public service has always been a big deal. I think I was dormant. When I was a kid I was awake to social inequality because of my lived experience, in Hackney, East London, in the eighties, nineties, you're nothing but awake, you're aware of your surroundings.[5] Then I went into my little IT bubble and had the protection of access to the stuff that many would see as indicators of success, such as company cars. I haven't got any money by the way! Those things that give you the illusion of success. When you put yourself back in the real world and stop wearing your shiny suits and your good shoes and you getting your hair cut five times a week or whatever, you're left with the reality. Education is one of the few institutions, a bit like the NHS, where you get to see people's lives stripped back. See the realness."*

Malcolm is a senior leader who is also active in the NEU. His experience as an organiser in a section of the union that some members don't even believe should exist has not been easy. These difficulties will be familiar to any leader who has run a project or worked within an organisation that they ultimately support and believe in, but that has aspects they wish to challenge and change for what they believe is the overall good:

---

5   According to local council policy documents, "Hackney is a culturally diverse area, with significant 'Other White', Black and Turkish/Kurdish communities". "Hackney was the eleventh most deprived local authority overall in England in the 2015 Index of Multiple Deprivation, whilst in 2010 it was ranked second." LB Hackney Policy Team, *A Profile of Hackney, its People and Place*, Document Number: 18909115 (January 2018). Available at: https://www.hackney.gov.uk/population?, p. 3, p. 4.

"I help organise and am a member of the Black Teachers Conference steering group. I'm the Black Officer for Devon – there was some, but not a massive amount of, competition for that gig.[6] I'm a co-founder of the South-West South Wales Black Teachers' Network. I do all kinds of stuff. I ask direct questions. I talk a lot about race. It has a conflict with my role as a senior leader but more a conflict with the NEU generally. In an equalities section like the Black Teachers we are beginning to have conversations about autonomy and self-determination, we are talking about changing some of the structures within the NEU and breaking down some of the barriers that exist. That is controversial to speak about in the first place because the NEU by definition is a trade union which is there to support all teachers, and you're talking about the inequalities that exist within it. Instantly that puts barriers up with a lot of people. There are some people within the union who don't necessarily agree with the idea of an equalities section for Black teachers and feel that equality means that there shouldn't be separate sections."

Malcolm explains how he wasn't sure how things were done when he first started his role in the union. He speaks of the importance of curiosity and of questioning structures and processes, even well-established ones. This can mean that you are seen as disruptive in the organisation that you are part of:

"We started off trial and error because there was nobody who gave us the handbook. There was no elder to tell us how this worked. We literally kicked in the door, waving the four-four.[7] We couldn't understand why things were done in a particular way and so asked direct questions or would question

---

6   In the south-west of England, where Malcolm is based, 4.9% of the teaching workforce are non-white British, compared to 13.7% nationally. This is the region with the second smallest percentage of non-white British teachers after the north-east (at 3%). These percentages will include other white groups such as White Irish, so the percentage of BAME teachers is possibly even lower that the quoted figures. Department for Education, Regional, LA and School Tables: School Workforce Census 2017 (28 June 2018). Available at: https://www.gov.uk/government/statistics/school-workforce-in-england-november-2017.

7   Malcolm is quoting a line which was originally delivered by the rapper the Notorious B.I.G. on hip hop classic "Get Money" by Junior M.A.F.I.A., taken from the album *Conspiracy*. We met at a HipHopEd event don't forget!

some of the structures and so on and so forth. I think the thing that both myself and my fellow organisers have in common is that we continue to ask the critical questions. That itch that is never ever going to go away. We are going to keep on asking, keep on asking, keep on asking."

Malcolm acknowledges the paradox of being both a member of the SLT, and thus part of the establishment of the organisation, while also being an individual who feels that some of the established norms of the school need to change. This view could potentially put you at odds with other members of the SLT:

"As a senior leader, an SLT member, you are part of the decision-making process of the school. That's your role and responsibility but at the same time, if you are an advocate of change, you want to change things and you could be in a conflicted position, potentially. In my role as an SLT member I sometimes have to remove myself from certain situations. There is a point of conflict where our influence and our roles kind of collide and there is a decision to be made. You have to decide whether you are SLT, therefore that's your job, you stand firm, or you support the agent of change or are the agent of change yourself."

Malcolm has worked in mainstream and alternative settings, in rural and urban environments. However, despite this seeming variety he is able to identify a common core to the types of schools he is drawn to work and lead in and the positions he has chosen to take. This relates back to what ultimately made him leave his corporate life to become a teacher:

"The common thread is definitely the factors or intersections of disadvantage. Disadvantage, when you think about it, is always about free school meals, pupil premium and all kinds of acronyms and terminology that's related to different types of funding. If I strip all of those away, and I often like to do that, then the intersections of disadvantage are often around where you live, your postcode, literally. It's about, in many cases, the racial profile of your family. It's about sexuality, about religious belief, about disability. It's about

all of the things that make any one person what they are. Those things, when they come into a classroom, act as factors of disadvantage."

As somebody who naturally challenges the status quo it might feel easier not to aspire to leadership or to avoid being in situations or roles where there may be disagreements with other decision makers. However, Malcolm is clear that disrupters must find a place for themselves in the decision-making process and in the rooms where key decisions are made if they want to affect real change:

"Statistically we know that someone who looks like me, from the background that I am from, does not necessarily get to be a senior leader.[8] It's about being in the room. When it comes to any decision-making process, if you are not in the room it doesn't matter what your opinion is, your voice is not heard. You need to be in the room, otherwise your voice is not part of the discussion, creating space for other voices who are not necessarily there. As an SLT member, you get your voice heard in lots of rooms, you definitely get to make decisions in some, and that is better than being on the outside of all of that and being a passive participant in the whole of that process."

What can we learn from Malcolm's story?

* Find people who will make you pause and reflect

If you are somebody who questions how and why your organisation does things a certain way, and wants to make change happen, it can sometimes be easy to rush into situations or new initiatives. Malcolm spoke about how he has benefited from having people around him in school who have made him less impulsive:

---

8   In secondary schools 6% of assistant head teachers or deputies are from BAME backgrounds and under 4% are head teachers. This is compared to roughly 10% of classroom staff and over 26% of students. Zubaida Haque and Sian Elliott, *Visible and Invisible Barriers: The Impact of Racism on BME Teachers* (London: Runnymede Trust and National Union of Teachers, 2016). Available at: https://www.teachers.org.uk/sites/default/files2014/barriers-report.pdf, p. 14.

"I can only talk about how it's worked out for me. In some instances you need an elder to show you the road. Within many of my roles I've been blessed to have been adopted by a mummy or a daddy in the workplace, who have given me some guidance or made me think. They haven't necessarily stopped me in every instance but they've made me pause and take a moment of reflection. An elder doesn't necessarily mean someone older than you, but someone who you respect. Throughout my education career, certainly, I've had someone to guide me in that way. Until now, where I'm on my own but then I'm building a network as well."

✳ Ask the question

Many people think that being a senior leader is about having the answers. This was certainly my view when I first started managing people. Malcolm turns that on its head. In his view, senior leaders need to be open to asking questions. I can confirm that I've met many leaders within and outside of education and the most impressive ones were not afraid to ask questions, especially ones that they didn't yet know the answers to themselves. Admitting that you don't know something, and showing that you are open to all ideas, takes bravery:

"I'm prepared to go and ask anybody the question that needs to be asked. I can do it humbly, I can do it harshly. Go ask the question. Putting yourself out there requires a level of vulnerability too ... Senior leaders ask the questions, you can ask the questions when you are outside the room, which gets you to being an SLT member, but when you are in the room you have to ask the right questions at the right time."

As Andrew Sobel and Jerold Panas write, "your job is to gain information and create vibrant dialogue" then, ultimately, to use this to help create the change you wish see in your organisation.[9]

---

9 Andrew Sobel and Jerold Panas, *Power Questions: Build Relationships, Win New Business, and Influence Others* (Hoboken, NJ: John Wiley and Sons, 2012), p. 85.

✳ Have a good reason to be disruptive

At its best and most effective, school leadership is not about you, or me, or whoever the leader is. It's about the lives that we can affect. Malcolm reminds us not to be disruptive and contrary for the sake of it. He suggests that it is a contrarian's duty to get into positions of authority and use that influence wisely to benefit others:

> "It's all about the people, it's all about the people, it's all about the people. You're doing it for yourself because you get paid to do the job, but you're doing it to aid people. That's the core principle that runs through everything. We make decisions that are for young people and they are for parents but we don't include them in that decision-making process and I think that's problematic. I'm not saying that every decision that's made has to include parental or young person consent but, at the same time, they are an important part of the conversation. That's guided my role as someone with pastoral responsibility because you're putting the kids first in every single decision you make."

✳ Find collaborators

Nobody ever heard of a one-person revolution. No matter how maverick you may think you are, you need allies. You need to work with people, even people who aren't an obvious fit. Malcolm was very clear on the need to collaborate as a leader, especially if you are suggesting ideas that may seem threatening to colleagues:

> "If you are naturally a disruptive force, collaborate first. With everybody. It makes you very vulnerable because people are going to steal your ideas, people are going to shut you down, people are going to dismiss your ideas or get you in the room and then downplay your ideas. Or they are going to really celebrate and embrace your ideas. You're going to bring the disruption anyway. But at least no one can say, 'Oh, you didn't include us.' As a disrupter, people are going to come at you whether you did it, you didn't do it or you think you might have done it. You apologise but they will still come at you. If

you come from a point of collaboration first, that noise is kind of reduced a little bit because you came, you waved the friendship banner, and then when you deal with people afterwards it's fine."

At my best I'm a natural collaborator and thrive when bouncing ideas around with others. However, I've noticed that if I'm feeling vulnerable or threatened I'm less likely to do this. My learning point here has been that the behaviour of other people should not be a reason to change positive habits that make you effective and happy, both professionally as a leader and as a human being.

✳ Everybody does politics

If you think that you can avoid internal politics as a senior leader, you are naive. You are as naive as I was when I first started. A former boss generously and patiently taught me to understand that not everybody was motivated by the same things as I was. If I thought that a particular change would ultimately end in better outcomes for students without a ridiculous increase in workload then I was all for it. It didn't matter whether I'd suggested it or not or if it meant getting rid of something that was established but no longer working. I assumed everyone else would be as willing to embrace change if it came with apparent benefits, but this proved not to be the case. This boss taught me to watch and listen to work out what drove the people I line managed, as well as colleagues in senior positions, and to use this to help me frame suggestions and requests. I didn't like this at first. Indeed, navigating internal politics is still something that I'm not entirely comfortable with. Malcolm's advice about politics within schools is essential for any leader who considers themselves unconventional in any way. You may think that you are above internal politics and want no part of it but your very existence as a school leader is political, so take Malcolm's advice:

> *"Being a senior leader is partly about your communication skills and your ability to manage experts in whatever your thing is, but it's just as important to be able to manage the politics of a school. The politics of a school are everything. You don't like doing it and you try not to be an active participant*

but you're in it because you're a senior leader and staff come to you and ask you questions, and those questions have agendas sometimes. Because they have agendas they have included you in the politics. You did not want to be in the politics but you are. You've got to accept it. Me, I'm a no-clique guy. But you've got to be aware of the cliques. The navigation of that is really difficult initially and it does, I think, become a skill that you need to have as part of your senior leader armoury."

✳ Find a variety of channels to get your voice heard

In leadership the most obvious way to get your voice heard is in meetings. Sometimes this works, sometimes it doesn't. Malcolm encourages us to fully understand the craft of leadership and influence as well as understanding the organisations we work in:

"You've got to know the system. Knowing your craft is knowing the system. In every school I've ever been in the secretary is probably the most important person in the building. Maybe speak to the secretary and say, 'I'd like to submit this.' The secretary is likely to look at what you're about to say and pass it to the right person, if they like you. So that's one of the ways."

✳ You can become a person of influence without a title

Sometimes people think that leadership is about titles. "Head" of this, "director" of that. In these roles you are certainly paid to have influence – but true influence is about whose behaviour you can affect, not just what the plaque on your office door says. I often meet teachers who don't feel they can change anything in their school because they don't have a leadership responsibility in their job title. Malcolm reminds us that we can be people of influence regardless of rank:

"In every school that I've ever seen or worked in, you've got a staff member who is the go-to person. It could be the person who all of the positive activity revolves around. It could be that lots of people go to that person because they

act as a confidant. If I think of Ms Brown in my first PRU, a lot of positive activity revolved around her, and she was quite a private person but, still, it revolved around her. When I met with her or connected with her, I realised that actually a lot of positive activity began occurring around me. I think she allowed me to step into the space to be the person of influence and that developed and grew. I was a learning assistant, I then became a teacher. I wasn't a deputy head teacher or an executive head teacher, or any of the senior roles in that particular school, but certainly I was the go-to person. So learning assistants with an issue would invariably come to me to ask for an opinion, guidance, suggestion, direction and so on and so forth. I didn't ask them to do that but clearly that's something that happened over a period of time. So in that school I was influential."

Parting words

As leaders we can't avoid playing politics and may find ourselves adapting to fit different situations. Malcolm's final words remind us of the importance of still being yourself as you don different roles:

"I'm a disrupter, which makes me problematic because disrupters shine brightly for a minute and then start causing problems. You have a particular shelf life. You need to be true to yourself, despite all of the different hats that you wear and the different performances of yourself that you apply in a school context – whether you're talking to a vulnerable kid or you're talking to someone you hate or you're talking to the cleaner. You are putting on different performances but all of these performances still are you and you need to remain true to yourself."

For Malcolm the sense of responsibility which comes with feeling like he stands for something bigger than himself drives him forward:

"I'm the exception, not the rule. I always come back to that. I always remember it. I guess because you are the exception you have a responsibility. I feel I have a responsibility to hold the door open to others."

CHAPTER 6

I value kindness, but I'm not a pushover – Karen's story

"I remember at my interview I said, 'Oh, I would like the staff to be happy' and they gave me a funny look."

You

* You believe in treating staff well and you want to develop them.

* You think that children ultimately benefit when the adults working with them are happy and empowered.

* However, you look around and see a narrative that tells you that leaders mustn't be too soft. They need to let staff know who is boss.

* People tell you that kind leaders are pushovers. Their schools aren't very good. Their teachers are only happy because they don't need to work hard and aren't very accountable and as a result students underperform.

* You wonder if there is a way to be a good leader of a successful school and a decent human being.

* You have a vision of a happy, skilled staff who get great outcomes for the children that they teach.

Read on to find out about an experienced head teacher who has proved that it is possible to turn a failing, undersubscribed school into a centre of excellence while improving staff morale.

Me

My first role as a head of department was difficult for me personally but helped shape my approach to how I treat staff and their development in two key ways. First, because my own working practices combined with the school environment eventually led to my major breakdown, as I mentioned in the introduction, I vowed that I would always strive to treat anybody I line managed or led in a way that respected their wellbeing and humanity while creating the conditions that enabled them to do their job well. In fact, for many years I had a homemade poster in my office reminding me, "Don't forget the goose". This was an allusion to the children's fairy tale of the goose that laid the golden egg and to a chapter in Stephen Covey's business classic, *The Seven Habits of Highly Successful People*, which was lent to me by a head I really respect.[1]

Second, for one year at that school, due to a massive budget deficit, all external continuing professional development (CPD) opportunities were banned. We were not allowed to go on any courses or generate cover in any way, apart from through sickness. However, middle leaders were each offered coaching and taught how to coach one another. This period taught me to look for the strengths within my team, to collaborate with other heads of department for interdepartmental training and to understand the different ways in which staff could be developed in a long-term and sustainable way beyond one-off courses. I also became obsessive about how we could share knowledge and learn as a department, as well as about critically evaluating my own leadership practice. This approach continued well into my time as an assistant head teacher and beyond. Additionally, because I took over a leadership role suddenly and unexpectedly, and then my breakdown forced someone else to take over from me, I have always favoured a sustainable approach to staff development that empowers anyone who is interested to do elements of the next role above them.

Karen

Karen has been the head teacher of a nursery school and children's centre in the east of England for over a decade and she describes herself as being "in the twilight years" of her teaching. Over the course of her forty-year career she has taught in London and the south-east of England, across primary and secondary phases. She has run a primary unit for children with emotional and behavioural difficulties, worked as an early years adviser for an inner London borough and as a home tutor for children with a terminal illness. Karen always has a smile on her face and the children she works with have described her as the "smiley and helpful office lady". Karen has supported many of her staff to become senior

---

1 Stephen R. Covey, *The Seven Habits of Highly Successful People: Powerful Lessons in Personal Change* (London: Simon & Schuster, 1989).

leaders, as well as working with external leaders to help them become more effective in their own settings. This is consistent with Karen's view that school leadership is about "growing leaders and growing learners".

I have known Karen for about six years. She is the head teacher of the nursery school and children's centre that all three of my children have attended.[2] For three years I was a community governor there and was able to witness the care and compassion she had for staff when making key decisions affecting the nursery. This is part of what made me want to send my own children there. As a parent, I also noted how happy, skilled and creative the staff were and the knock-on effect that had on the learning and wellbeing of my children, and all their peers.

The nursery is hugely popular in our local area and Karen is often asked to share good practice within the county and beyond. She is a vocal advocate for the early years sector, and has sat on national committees and mentored other leaders. Karen has been a head teacher for over ten years and, in that time, has taken the nursery from a place where not many families wanted to send their children to a shining beacon. She's done it while being a thoroughly decent person. The working environment she has created is the physical embodiment of what Mary Myatt captures in the title of one of my favourite books about organisational culture, *High Challenge, Low Threat*.[3]

Karen's personal experience of education meant she left school feeling that not much was expected of her and her career prospects:

> *"It was the classic thing in my day, 'Oh girls, you can be a secretary or go and work in an office.' Nobody considered that I would go to university and I went to a college of education by default really. I went to college and found out*

---

2   Children's centres, sometimes called Sure Start centres, provide a physical hub for a range of services aimed at children aged 0–5 and their families. The nursery shared a site with a range of other facilities in the children's centre. At times Karen refers to the nursery and children's centre interchangeably.

3   Mary Myatt, *High Challenge, Low Threat: How the Best Leaders Find the Balance* (Woodbridge: John Catt Educational, 2016).

about psychology and sociology and how we develop as humans. It made me really believe that teaching is a great privilege because we are enabling everybody else to learn, but it's so important that we are learning ourselves. Or else you are in a terrible rut or routine and your expectations are lowered."

Karen started her career in the secondary sector, teaching maths and English to children with special educational needs (SEN). But she eventually made the decision to move phases to impact children at the very start of their educational journey. She was very clear about why she wanted to make the change of phase and be the head teacher of a nursery school:

"Why do I do it? Oh, golly! To make a difference to children. In my current role, as head teacher of a nursery school, I can make a difference to a lot of children and families. Not only here for the children who come to the nursery but also with the children's centre and more generally across the county, because I also represent the voice of early years at various groups and forums. I started teaching in secondary schools, where I taught children with significant emotional and behavioural difficulties. That was a great job – really, really challenging – and I was very successful. Then I realised that, for me, it's more important to work with younger and younger children."

Learning and development is at the core of everything that Karen does for the children and staff:

"Obviously, learning is the basis of everything that we are doing with our children. I think every child has probably far more potential and possibilities for learning than we can possibly imagine. Learning without limits is really important. I think that we sometimes don't realise what we can achieve ourselves as adults and what children can achieve. At Oaktree, we make sure that learning is fun, interesting and inspiring, and that it is adapted to individual children. We also believe that all children can do amazingly well."

Karen's values and vision have been on display since before she became a head teacher. She brought an unusual physical prop to her headship interview and combined this with her love of gardening to create a strong vision and image for the future of what became her nursery school:

> "I remember saying at my interview that I wanted the nursery to be a flagship, a centre of excellence. The early years adviser on my interview panel was visibly sceptical, 'Oh, really?' The school wasn't doing that well back then. I had this vision: a tree. I took a conker along to my interview, and I talked about how that would grow and how the school and the children's centre were the trunk and the branches growing out were the communities, the branches and the leaves were the families, and the children were all the conkers. It was quite a visual image they could tie into. It is still my vision now. Over time it's changed and the children have become acorns instead of conkers. The tree is an oak tree, to match what we renamed the children's centre. All of the children are the acorns. It's through them, hopefully, that those early experiences that we have had with them will be spread in myriad places, throughout their lives. The vision is that the children will develop a love of learning and we, as staff, will too."

Perhaps because Karen was not expected to go to university, she was always striving to take advantage of any opportunity to learn and improve in order to have more of an impact with the children and families that she worked with. A self-described "course junkie", who other colleagues sometimes gently teased accordingly, Karen's own professional development and love of learning was encouraged by a boss she had earlier in her career. This experience eventually helped to shape Karen's own approach to staff development:

> "The head of the school very much supported me. I didn't always see eye to eye with her but she supported my, and another enthusiastic colleague's, professional development and funded me to do a master's in education at Cambridge. She let me have time out to study and showed that she believed

that what I was doing there was making a big difference. I'd gone to a college of education and I had got a degree but I'd never really thought that I was particularly able. Then I started doing my master's and it was really, really, really hard but I achieved it. So that made me think, if I can do that anybody can really. It really made me think that we can all do amazing things but you have to trust people and put your beliefs into action. When I became a head myself, that was one of my key things. I wanted a high level of professional development for my staff so that they could also experience that growth, confidence and self-belief, that encouragement. 'Yup, you can do it.'"

Karen became a head teacher after working as a local authority adviser, a role that Lila and Tait – who we met in Chapters 3 and 4 – also occupied during their careers. She had never been a deputy, so experienced some challenges when she was first appointed head. However, over time, she started to make progress with a core team of staff:

"I hadn't had much experience of dealing with challenging issues or confrontation among staff. I spent the first year thinking, 'Why did I do this?' A lot of staff who had been there a long time left and I appointed a lot of new staff, so there was a lot of change. I remember one person saying, 'I think you're exactly the right person to do this job, Karen, but I can't stay here and do it with you.' They didn't have the energy because they'd been used to not working very hard. Some just drifted away. Luckily, we built a strong team. We made some key appointments. I think a lot of leadership is about having the right people around you, isn't it? The governors were also really supportive. In fact, recently one of our ex-governors has become one of our practitioners, which is lovely. The staff who stayed, like our school business manager, encouraged me and were always super positive. They could see what my vision was for the school."

Karen knew that for the nursery to become the centre of excellence that she knew it could be, there would need to be a change in ethos and practice, and that started with her own example to the staff:

"When I started, I didn't realise that the school had been causing concern. There were lots of challenges, not least the whole school was a mess. The staff were skilled but there were very low levels of wellbeing. A very high absence rate. It wasn't very popular, we had low numbers of children. And to top it all they'd had an acting head for a term who'd kind of exacerbated all those factors and made everything very divisive. There was a lot to do. The head should be the lead learner. Always learning new things. That's why I like to go to lots of different groups, read articles and go to conferences because unless you and the staff are really highly skilled and alert and confident in your roles, you can't possibly deliver a good curriculum for the children. I think that just wasn't happening before I arrived. There were good practitioners there, but they hadn't done anything. They didn't go on courses. They were totally inward-looking and stagnated."

The early years sector is traditionally less well paid and has proportionally more staff with a lower level of formal education compared to compulsory primary and secondary education.[4] Karen herself is no stranger to prejudices about working in the early years:

---

4   Comparing Sarah Bonetti, *The Early Years Workforce: A Fragmented Picture* (London: Education Policy Institute, 2018). Available at: https://epi.org.uk/publications-and-research/early-years-workforce_analysis/, pp. 18–23, and Department for Education, School Workforce in England: November 2017. Bonetti (p. 19) shows that 7–26% of early years foundation stage (EYFS) staff who were not senior managers had a qualification that was degree level (level 6) or above. Taking senior managers into account, this changes to 10–40%, depending on the setting. This is in contrast with DfE data stating that approximately 95% of teachers in state maintained schools (excluding nurseries) having Qualified Teacher Status (and by implication at least a degree or equivalent since you must have a level 6 qualification to be awarded QTS) (Table 3a). According to Bonetti (p. 14), pay range for non-senior EYFS staff is generally £8–13 per hour. For a forty-hour work week, and a forty-eight-week working year, this would be the equivalent of £15,360–24,960 p.a. This is compared with DfE data that gives median yearly salary as approximately £31,000–36,000 for primary classroom teachers and approximately £36,000–39,000 for secondary classroom teachers (Table 9b). There are further variations according to age and gender.

"When I graduated from my master's degree we were all in the garden, having our champagne, and it was all so lovely. A parent of another person on the course said, 'Oh, where do you work?' and I said, 'I work in a nursery school with children under 5.' And she said, 'Oh, surely you're wasted there?' And I thought, 'No, actually, for me, working with children under 5 is the most important place to be teaching. This is where it makes a difference.'"

Karen is passionate about creating opportunities for all of her staff to become more skilled and to help them make a difference. Ultimately, investing in staff benefits the children they teach and the wider communities they are part of:

"Early education and early years practitioners are traditionally seen as girls who leave school with limited qualifications. 'There's nothing else you can do, go and work with young children.' I hate that view. I want all of my staff to be regarded as professionals. I love that everyone calls them teachers. Nobody really knows who the teachers are and who the early years assistants are.

"If I can see that a member of staff will really be good at something, I give them the opportunity. I was talking to one of our teaching assistants (TAs) the other day, who left school at 14. When I started as head teacher she wasn't the best TA, but we discovered that she was brilliant with children with SEN, and particularly autism, because she has a lot of experience with it in her family. Suddenly we realised, 'Wow! You are actually brilliant.' So then I said, 'Go on this course. Go on that training.' It's about finding the best pathway for people, always believing that they can develop and obviously giving them time. Lots of our staff have already got early years teacher qualifications and have moved on to roles with more responsibility. I hope that soon some of them will become heads or senior leaders themselves. I also love seeing the staff who started as parent helpers and are now early years practitioners.

"We've got lots of different opportunities to impact across the lives of young children and their families. If staff have potential but are not quite in the right role, I think, 'Maybe this isn't the right slot for you, let's have another think

about where your strengths lie and what training, development or support you need from other colleagues to help you move forward.' It makes staff talent-spot each other but it also makes them talent-spot the children and that's obviously what matters. Now we've got a couple of staff on maternity leave, so I've said to others, 'Yes, you can step up into that role.' They want to. They embrace the challenge."

At the core of Karen's approach is sharing knowledge and empowering all of her staff, whatever their current title. For her, this should be an ongoing process, which benefits everybody, as the base level of skills and knowledge in her organisation continues to rise:

"I think it's really important for staff to stay fresh, that's why I wanted the teaching school status.[5] It gives everybody the opportunity to be part of ongoing learning. I think the training or courses which have a real impact are those which last over time.[6] I've tried to send people on sustained courses – training that lasts for a few weeks, a few months, a few years, even. You can get lovely ideas from going for a day's training but it won't be embedded. I also try to have two or three people doing the same thing at the same time if possible, because then they can co-facilitate that with the rest of the staff.

"My master's was very influential for me, as was the advanced diploma that I did when I was a very young teacher. When some of the nursery school staff started their foundation degrees, they said things like, 'Now I'm confident that

---

5 Teaching schools are officially recognised centres of excellence that tend to coordinate teacher training and school-to-school support to help improve other local schools. See the DfE's guidance to applicants for more details: https://www.gov.uk/guidance/teaching-schools-a-guide-for-potential-applicants#role-of-teaching-schools.

6 A meta-analysis of a range of research studies conducted by CUREE found that effective CPD for teachers that was more likely to improve student outcomes involved "enquiry oriented learning activities spread over (usually) two terms or more". Philippa Cordingley and Miranda Bell, *Understanding What Enables High Quality Professional Learning: A Report on the Research Evidence* (CUREE and Pearson School Improvement, 2012). Available at: http://www.curee.co.uk/publication/understanding-what-enables-high-quality-professional-learning, p. 8.

what I was doing was the right thing.' Traditionally, early years practitioners are not always the most highly educated and don't necessarily have to understand the philosophical and pedagogical reasons behind why they do things, but now they have extra confidence. So having people doing courses at that high level was great and then we appointed a member of staff who was doing her PhD and she was also a brilliant role model for people."

Karen wants her staff to be confident and competent enough to feel that they can make a real difference, individually and collectively, for the children in the Oaktree community:

"We are doing a great thing called teacher-led development at the moment, which we've opened up to all practitioners. It's run throughout the year and it's about making the difference to young children. Last year we had three people doing it and they introduced yoga into the school. They introduced sensory play. They looked at engaging parents. It's really about taking on a leadership role within a school. For some people that's a really challenging thing to do but they found it really empowering. It fosters self-awareness and creates space for reflection because you realise you are a person who can make a difference. I'm so proud because one of the people who did it last year has gone on to do the same master's degree I did. She's the first person on the course from a children's centre, which is really great to see."

In a time of squeezed budgets, many head teachers and school leaders may baulk at paying for external CPD or allowing teaching staff out of school for extended periods of time due to costs. Karen was clear that this short-term thinking needs to be challenged. Her approach of trusting, developing and empowering staff has had amazing results in a phase where high staff turnover is an issue:[7]

---

7   According to the National Day Nurseries Association (NDNA), 86% of survey respondents had experienced staff losses in 2017. National Day Nurseries Association, *NDNA 2017/18 Workforce Survey* (2018). Available at: https://www.ndna.org.uk/NDNA/News/Reports_and_surveys/Workforce_survey/Workforce_survey_2018.aspx, p. 5.

"Practitioners learning and seeing each other develop has been fantastic for them and fantastic for the children. Many, many schools have a huge recruitment crisis for early years practitioners, but we hadn't had a supply teacher for three years before this term. Michael Wilshaw was reported as saying, 'If anyone says to you that "staff morale is at an all-time low" you know you are doing something right ...'[8] I don't believe that at all. I remember at my interview I said, 'Oh, I would like the staff to be happy', and they gave me a funny look. One of the things we focused on when I arrived was staff wellbeing. They've got to feel fulfilled and confident. We've done staff wellbeing questionnaires for the last few years and the first one was quite bad. And then it made a huge improvement and has continued to be really good.

"Recruiting a new practitioner from scratch is very expensive. We're going to support one of our early years practitioners who's got her BA degree to do her initial teacher training and pay both her salary and her training fees because it's a short-term investment for a long-term gain. We know she's going to be brilliant and if we had to recruit a teacher from somewhere else we'd have to do their induction. They'd probably be more expensive because they'd be higher up the scale. You don't even know that they are going to be any good."

Karen wasn't particularly happy about having to justify these decisions in economic terms, but acknowledged that it is the reality we are operating within. She was also clear about the benefits of feeling empowered and valued on morale, sickness and attendance, which ultimately has a knock-on effect on children's learning:

"If you want staff's attendance rates to be good you can justify the cost of CPD. You only have to have a member of staff absent for four or five days

---

8   Quoted in Fran Abrams, Is the New Chief Inspector of Schools Just an Instrument of Government?, *The Guardian* (23 January 2012). Available at: https://www.theguardian.com/education/2012/jan/23/chief-inspector-schools-michael-wilshaw.

and that's the equivalent of a £400 course for us. Making good appointments and recruiting staff is the single most important thing a head does. You can recruit the best person in the world but if they're not given the opportunities to develop and use their skills then they become not very effective. Our staff don't have to stay with us at all. They could go and get a much better paid job somewhere else but they love the ethos here. They love the children and they love the teamwork too.

"If we weren't outward-facing we would have gone a long time ago. I think nursery schools are always under threat. So you always have to look out. 'What's the next opening? What's the next possibility?' So that's a driver because if you don't continually improve then you would shrivel, but you need to be looking at the wider picture for the good of your families, for the good of your children."

At the time of writing, England is still in the midst of a teacher recruitment and retention crisis. The government has missed its training targets for newly qualified teachers (NQTs) five years in a row and large numbers of working-age teachers are leaving the profession.[9] As a school leader you may not have control over factors such as funding but you can influence the ethos, climate and working culture of your school. Respecting, empowering and valuing staff in the way that Karen has may, over time, lead to greater satisfaction as you create the space for individuals to have a tangible impact on the lives of the children they teach.[10]

---

9   Jack Worth, The UK's Teacher Supply Is Leaking … and Fast, *TES* [blog] (28 June 2018). Available at: https://www.tes.com/news/uks-teacher-supply-leaking-and-fast.
10 Research by the think tank LKMco states that "Teachers primarily stay in the profession because they feel good at it and that they are having an impact." Loic Menzies et al., *Why Teach?* (LKMco and Pearson, 2015). Available at: http://whyteach.lkmco.org/wp-content/uploads/2015/10/Embargoed-until-Friday-23-October-2015-Why-Teach.pdf, p. 16.

What can we learn from Karen's story?

✳ Train your staff to spot talent in others

It's not possible for a leader to know everything but Karen has empowered all of her staff to notice strengths in their peers:

> "I'm not always the person who spots opportunities for staff. Often it's somebody else who says, 'Oh Karen, X has done something amazing in this area and is really interested in it.' So my job is to say, 'Yep, okay. Let's just support them with doing that.'"

I used to have a boss who would ask me to tell her about a specific action that each member of my team should be acknowledged for when she and I had our regular line management meetings. Initially I thought this was cheesy, but people really liked being recognised, whether by email, a card or a quick mention from a passing SLT member in the corridor. This is a practice that I carried on myself as an assistant head.

✳ Remember to constantly bring staff on the journey with you

Karen was clear that it's not enough to tell staff the vision that you have for them and for your school just once. It needs to be revisited regularly. This is something that I know I could have been better at as a senior leader. I could definitely have learnt from what Karen had to say:

> "In our centre, we have had a lot of very fortuitous changes. People have to be flexible. We have recently taken over three more children's centres. With every change, revisioning is important. When we were designated first as a national support school and then as a teaching school, I asked staff, 'Okay, what does this mean to you?' It's important to remember that while it's perhaps clear in my head, or for the staff who've been there a long time, you have to revisit it for most other people."

Development and growth is a journey. Staff need to know what they are working towards. In the busy lives of schools the big picture can be lost, especially with deadlines to be met and with natural changes of staff. Regular reminders can help to reinspire people, as well as help the school community to see their progress and help new staff to buy into the ethos.

* A happy, fulfilled staff affects your budget

At the time of writing, schools in England are facing increasingly tight budgets. Many are choosing a variety of efficiency methods, including giving staff more teaching hours, reducing training budgets and asking staff to pay for staffroom refreshments. My own school is about to move from printed reports to electronic ones, which will reduce printing costs over the year by thousands of pounds. Karen was clear that, in her view, having a fulfilled staff is the number one thing that a head teacher can do:

> *"The most important thing for the budget is the staffing, getting the people with the right skills and the right attitude. Everything else falls into place."*

In schools with low morale, staff absence and turnover is high – and Karen explained how this has a monetary effect. "You waste thousands and thousands on supply staff." This is before considering the disruption to the children's learning. Investing money in staff, beyond what it initially costs to hire them, and their development may seem like an extra but it's essential. Fulfilled staff turn up for work consistently and will go the extra mile for you and for the communities they serve.

* Don't be a pushover

Being fair and treating staff well is not the same as being a pushover. Karen tries to be considerate to staff but she is clear that she will not let people take advantage of this:

"People are always asking, 'Can I do this? Can I go half an hour early for this? Can I do that?' Often I have to say, 'No you can't.' It's not always about saying 'yes' to everything. Demonstrating fairness will help people to respect your judgement."

✳ Model development yourself

Learning is clearly a core value for Karen. As a leader it is important to model your core values and have the same expectations of yourself as of your staff:

"We have this whole scheme called Watch a Friend and I've just had one practitioner from another setting arrive with us and she said, 'I've been working in early years for nineteen years, I don't need to Watch a Friend.' I replied, 'Yes you do, everybody in this school takes part: the senior teachers, me, we learn so much from each other.'"

Continuous learning at all levels has such great benefits for the children. I share Karen's view that it is at the core of what creates a successful school.

Parting words

Some leaders and organisations worry about developing staff, watching them grow and flourish, only to have them leave. This can be frustrating, but Karen takes a system-wide view, saying, "That's fine. They need to take great elements of our school and apply them to another setting." Having excellent staff leave can benefit other schools in the system – and so benefit more children – so it's not a problem, as long as they have achieved what you want them to in your setting first. Karen traced her own desire to develop her staff back to the boss who had funded her master's degree earlier in her career:

"She very much supported my professional development and funded me to do a master's degree. She created staff meetings where I could talk

about my research – feeding back about the difference it was making to the children. She created a new role for me. She really did influence me, always encouraging, providing opportunities."

Karen takes a broad view, wanting to ensure that all her staff can benefit from the kinds of opportunities that have been afforded to her and that everyone embraces the ethos of growth and development; embedding it within the school but also taking it with them if they do move on. In this way, Karen's influence and values extend far beyond her own school gates. Opportunities that I have received led to me supporting and coaching other leaders who have then gone on to lead teams of their own. In our own way, both Karen and I are doing what we can to "hold the door open" for school leaders after us, as Malcolm suggested in Chapter 5. I hope this book will offer support to current leaders who are looking for an alternative narrative about being effective while being true to who they are. So follow Karen's lead and take time to help and support people at all levels in your organisation – you have no idea what impact they may have in the future.

PART III

BEYOND

Beyond

Students are often shocked to bump into their teachers outside of school in the evening or at the weekend. It's almost like they think we are locked in a cupboard when they leave in the afternoon, which opens up again just before they return the next day. Sometimes long hours and high workloads can make us feel as though that might as well be true; leadership is hugely rewarding but it can also take a lot from us, both at work and in our personal lives. For some of us, at times, our lives beyond the school gates will inevitably affect how we feel about our experiences inside, as well as our perceptions of our work. This is the side of school leadership that is rarely discussed publicly and, as a consequence, too many of us suffer silently. It doesn't need to be this way.

CHAPTER 7

I am more than my job title – Allana's story

"I think, within myself, I was really unhappy with having my life all-encompassed by work. So it came down to, 'What are the things that I can change?'"

You

∗ You have a strong purpose for coming in every day, for planning those lessons, marking those books, developing those you line manage.

∗ You enjoy your job. Possibly not every tiny detail – and you could do without the admin – but you absolutely know why you teach, why you stay and why you lead, or why you want to.

∗ You are generally proud of what you do and you feel good knowing that you are making a difference to young people.

∗ But there is something nagging away at you.

∗ Maybe you are seeing less of your friends. Perhaps you can't remember the last time you met for a night out or let your hair down.

∗ Perhaps you have a gym membership you've hardly used this year or a club or evening class that you've been missing because you have been too busy.

∗ Maybe you've not finished the end of a film or a TV series because every time you sit down on the sofa in the evenings you fall asleep.

∗ Perhaps you've had to pull over on the drive home from work more than once because you felt your eyelids drooping.

∗ Maybe you've realised that it's been a month since you were last home for your children's bedtime.

∗ Maybe it dawns on you on your commute that you have not spoken to your partner for longer than ten minutes at a time for several days. Maybe you don't have a partner because you never have time to meet anyone.

∗ If you recognise any of the above scenarios, which have happened to me, then this chapter is for you.

Leadership is rewarding but it can be difficult. Leaders are generally expected to work long hours and often, because of the types of people we are, happily choose to anyway. You want to do your job well, but know that you also need to create space for the activities, people and experiences that nourish you outside of work.

Me

Teachers can feel guilty about setting boundaries around when and for how long they work. In the DfE's workload survey, almost one-quarter of full-time teachers reported that 40% of their total working hours were outside of school time.[1] This can be magnified for teachers who are in leadership positions; SLT members report working a sixty-hour week on average, compared to a fifty-four-hour week for classroom teachers and middle leaders.[2] I once coached a middle leader from another school who worried that her team worked too hard and that they were going to burn out. I asked her what example she set and she admitted that she often marked late into the night and that her health and personal life were suffering. According to the Trades Union Congress (TUC) she is not alone: "Chief executives work the most unpaid hours on average each week (13.1 hours). They are closely followed by teachers and education professionals (12.1 hours per week)."[3] This is over the forty-eight-hour limit of the EU working time directive. Surely if she worked like that then her team – who liked and respected her – would think that was the model to emulate, was my challenge to her. She reflected and decided to change her own behaviour so her team felt they had permission to make the time to enjoy their lives beyond work.

Having interests beyond work does not mean that your work and personal life need to be completely separate. There is not always a clear and fixed divide.

---

1   Will Hazell, Teachers Work a 54-Hour Week, DfE Survey Finds, *TES* (24 February 2017). Available at: https://www.tes.com/news/teachers-work-54-hour-week-dfe-survey-finds.
2   John Higton et al., *Teacher Workload Survey 2016: Research Report* (London: Department for Education, 2017). Available at: https://assets.publishing.service.gov.uk/government/uploads/system/uploads/attachment_data/file/592499/TWS_2016_FINAL_Research_report_Feb_2017.pdf.
3   TUC, Workers in the UK Put in £33.6 Billion Worth of Unpaid Overtime a Year, Trades Union Congress [press release] (24 February 2017). Available at: https://www.tuc.org.uk/news/workers-uk-put-%C2%A3336-billion-worth-unpaid-overtime-year.

Life isn't like that. Leaders do have to put in extra work and have more responsibilities, it's why we get paid more. However, if we have work that we enjoy and feel is meaningful, we can do our best in our role and make the decision to have clear boundaries around the time that belongs to us beyond work. It looks different for different people, and sometimes we need the help of our family, friends and extended professional networks to keep us on track, but it can be done.

An integrated life with elements beyond our day jobs can recharge and refresh us so that ultimately we have more energy when we are at work. By demonstrably balancing our priorities we also give our teams permission to do so and act as good role models. Overall, this makes for happier organisations. Not everything can or should be compartmentalised. Ideally our experiences at work will enrich us as people and our experiences and interests beyond work will influence how we approach our careers and teaching.

I have generally enjoyed the different roles that I've held but there came a significant turning point when I realised that my work had become all-consuming in a way that was unhealthy and unsustainable. The signs that something was wrong were there for some time but I ignored them until I could do so no longer. I didn't want to be seen as uncommitted to my job so I worked harder and harder, my sleep became more and more irregular and my personal relationships became more and more strained. Eventually, perhaps inevitably, this became too much and I was forced to stop (as I outlined in the preface).

While I was off work recovering, I started to look after myself better and took daily exercise. I also realised I wanted to make regular time and space for other things in my life. Two very obvious ones were my partner and our son, who was a toddler at the time, but I also realised that I needed something specifically for myself that wasn't related to work or to anybody else.

I discovered my own personal source of joy accidently. An incredibly kind colleague, William, taught me to paint while I was recovering from my breakdown. During an ill-fated attempt to return to work, I was temporarily in school on a reduced timetable and he offered me space in the back of his art classroom to paint when I wasn't teaching in the afternoons. I wasn't very good but I realised that I loved creating visual art and so I took up photography. Several years later, an interest in photography has turned into a love of helping people to tell their own stories, to help themselves and others, as well as a way of helping me to explore questions that I have about life. Indirectly it led to me writing this book. Creativity brings me joy and I now know I have to make time for it within and beyond my job. Whatever your own personal passion or motivation is, change starts with the realisation that your current working patterns may not be allowing you much room for the other things in your life.

Allana

Allana has been teaching for fifteen years and is currently a head teacher in a primary school in North London. The majority of her career has been spent teaching maths and sciences to students in secondary schools in the capital, but more recently she has shifted phases. Allana is in her late thirties and was born on the Caribbean island of Trinidad, where the majority of her family still live. She moved to the UK to study at university, as did her sister. Reflecting on her childhood memories, she says her favourite way to spend a Sunday afternoon is, "on a beach or sleeping and dreaming of a beach". Allana is passionate about education because she wants to give her students the opportunity to stretch themselves to go beyond what might be expected of them given their family background. Her own mother, despite only being educated up to primary school level, pushed Allana and her siblings by taking them to extra lessons in subjects they needed help with, but Allana knows that a lot of her students don't benefit from this support at home and wants to provide an education that gives them everything they need to excel. Allana's students would describe her as "strict, funny and fair" and she describes school leadership as "a journey of hidden bravery with the highest stakes possible". Despite a crushing and almost career-ending experience she had at a previous school, where she worked hard and for long hours as a senior leader, she is optimistic about education and feels that the system is on "a journey of change".

Allana used to regularly put in thirteen-hour days on the school site before going home to continue her work. She has subsequently built a life with very clear boundaries around how she works, alongside making more time for her family and focusing on progressing in her career on her own terms. She explains that chemistry is her favourite subject to teach "because I used to fail at it", which gives us a real insight into Allana's character. At different points in her life and career she has turned negative experiences into chances to reflect, change direction and reinvent herself. She's also committed to improving the experiences of other leaders.

In the years between our first meeting, at an education conference, and our interview, external factors had forced Allana to radically rethink the prominence that she gave work in her life:

> "I had started at a new school. It was open to staff until nine o'clock at night as well as on Saturdays and Sundays. It was a school in crisis. We had no head teacher at that point in time. The SLT were in friction because you had old SLT and then new SLT, which I was part of, so everybody was up against it. I worked and I worked and I worked because I wanted the school to do well. So I kept working. The caretakers would put me out at nine o'clock at night and I'd keep going at home, and then I'd rock up the next day. At some point I realised, 'Actually, I don't see my child. He's got a lot going on with his own life and I'm not there to attend most of it or to be a part of it.' His grandparents filled in really well but it still wasn't fair to him. I'd leave home on a Saturday and say, 'Alright, I'm going to school now.'"

Despite this dedication, the school continued to struggle and Allana came in one day to some shocking news:

> "We had an SLT meeting the day before the Easter break and the governors walked in and said, 'We've taken a decision to make all of you redundant.' They fired all of us on the last day before the Easter holidays."

This sudden blow came at a time when Allana's life really needed some stability:

"My mother was dying of cancer, we'd reached our last remission stage and we were going in to the doctor telling us, 'Well, this cycle, we can't continue. She's getting older. It's taking its toll. We can't just keep on with chemotherapy and keep on with everything else.'"

Allana's mother had been a seminal figure in her life and had helped shape her educational philosophy:

"My mum was only educated up to primary level and she never went beyond that. After school she was a servant for somebody and she went to work as a maid in their house. She didn't want us to go through what she went through because of a lack of education. She'd ask us, 'What do you need help in? You need lessons in maths? Let's go here.' She'd be ferrying us around and making us do that extra work because of her own experience. 'You need lessons in chemistry? Yes, you do, you just don't know you need it yet. We're going here.' She didn't know how to make us better herself but she knew that if she accessed all these different people, those teachers would know how to make us better. I want our education system here in England to have that sort of access."

Sadly, Allana's mother was ill for some time, having been diagnosed when she came to visit Allana after the birth of her son:

"My mum came from Trinidad to visit us in England when my son was born. She was feeling ill, tired and run down. It was the six-month check for the baby and I said, 'I'm going to the doctor. You can come along and we'll see if they can see you.' When he saw her, he looked at her, listened to the symptoms and said, 'I think it's multiple myeloma,' which is a type of leukaemia. When it was diagnosed I said to her, 'You can't go anywhere.' I started the application process for her to stay in the UK. For the application to be approved you have to be secure in a job, you have to have a source of income to pay for the treatments and to get everything started. After that, I think, my progression to leadership happened. Mum went into remission a couple of times. Every time

she got a bit better I'd slow down on working. Then she'd worsen so I'd go back into it, working really hard and putting in the hours."

Allana had been working extremely hard as an assistant head teacher in a tough school when she was made redundant, and for a while the experience shook her faith in the sector she'd dedicated so much time and effort to:

"To me that was a painful experience of how education can be. I wanted to leave teaching because I thought, 'That's so cruel and harsh. I can't do this any more. There is no point. I've put everything into this and there is no appreciation.' Future Leaders was the network that talked me through the experience and its aftermath and said, 'No, no, no, that's one school. One experience. You need to put everything in perspective.'[4] Richard, our leadership coach, visited and said, 'Let's see what we can do here.' He helped me back up to regain the confidence to go out and apply for new jobs. He started making me question what I was are doing and I thought, 'Okay, maybe I can make this a little better.' The lotto numbers didn't come in at any point so you need to dust yourself off. You pick yourself up and you say, 'Right, I have to find a way to make this work.' I'd done primary to secondary transition when I was at my previous school and I'd always thought it would be nice to be in a primary school for a year. Somebody at Future Leaders said to me, 'Would you consider doing a placement in a primary school?' and I said, 'Yeah, sure.' They said, 'Well, think of it as a blossoming. Try something you always wanted to try.' If it weren't for them, I'd have left this career by now."

Allana found that she enjoyed leading in a primary school and she stayed on as a deputy head teacher for longer than the year her original placement required. She has even tried to persuade me to switch to the primary sector on more than one occasion telling me, "Primaries are the bomb!" Additionally, Allana's previous experience has made her much clearer about how she wants to live her life:

----

4   Now known as Ambition School Leadership, see https://www.ambitionschoolleadership.org.uk/.

"After that I thought, 'You know what? I place value on what I do for the kids and I place value on what I do in order to promote the school, but I'm not going to let it switch my work–life balance to the extent that I'm slaving away for the school but I'm not able to give to those who genuinely love, treasure and appreciate me.' Since then, there's been a change! I think, within myself, I was really unhappy with having my life all-encompassed by work. So it came down to, 'What are the things that I can change?'"

What can we learn from Allana's story?

✳ Set clear boundaries for yourself and others

The government has recognised and acknowledged issues around teacher workload and the DfE has issued policy papers outlining plans to "remove unnecessary workload for teachers, so they can focus on teaching and their own development".[5] However, you can't wait for external forces to take effect. While welcome, these plans aren't going to make your workload more sustainable today or this week. Allana's working practices have changed drastically from her days of weekends at work and evenings on site until nine o'clock. Her current primary school has daily practices that communicate expectations about reasonable working hours.

> *"The caretaker locks up at six o'clock. He comes round and says, 'The cleaners are done. What are you still doing here? Get out.'"*

My current head teacher has teenage children and generally leaves work at around 5 p.m. so that he can spend time with his family. He lives nearby and is in at around 8 a.m. This communicates a powerful message to staff. Yes, he

---

5 Department for Education, Reducing Teacher Workload: Policy Paper (24 July 2018). Available at: https://www.gov.uk/government/publications/reducing-teachers-workload/reducing-teachers-workload.

works hard and sometimes has to return for functions in the evening, but by leaving work at a reasonable time he shows everyone that we can do so too, if we wish, and that we can manage our workload as we see fit. As an assistant head, I worked fairly long hours in the week but I always left by 3.45 p.m. on a Friday to take my son to karate. I was clear with colleagues why I wouldn't be available on Friday afternoons and this was always respected. It's okay to have a life and commitments beyond work.

Being a school leader is demanding. We start early with meetings and can have very long days if there are after-school functions to attend, but we can still make time for the other things that are important in our lives, with some commitment and imagination.

✳ Make time for networks and relationships outside your school

Allana is certain that without her wider professional networks, such as WomenEd[6] and Future Leaders, she would not have been able to recover from the disappointment and shock of being made redundant:

> "I think external networks are what make leaders. Build your network far outside your school because there is far more support available outside. Your external network are the ones you turn to. They can provide the opportunities for the next big thing or even the next small thing in your life and career. It comes from a cup of coffee, sitting down in a cafe somewhere, and having that moment to just offload and take advice. That comes from an external network."

I can echo Allana's words. It is essential to find peers who you can turn to for advice when necessary. I remember one day at work when I was feeling overwhelmed, I called my friend Emma, a fellow senior leader who was working

---

6 See http://www.womened.org/.

at a school nearby. She met me later the same day, bringing sandwiches and offering a kind, supportive and neutral ear. I was able to regroup and see the situation in a different and more objective way. Simple gestures of support can mean so much when things feel like they are getting on top of you. I first met Emma on a training course for school leaders in our local area; external training is one opportunity to grow your network and connect with like-minded peers beyond your school.

✳ Consider what workaholism is making you miss

Allana was forced to re-evaluate the proportion of her life that work consumed because of sudden redundancy. She realised that spending a disproportionate amount of time at work would affect the limited time she had with her terminally ill mother. She also wanted to spend more time with her teenage son:

> "Before, I'd think, 'I need to get the work done.' Now I need to get things done for him and then look at my workload."

You don't have to make massive changes, just finding a bit of time to do something that's important to you can be transformative. During a busy period, I worried about the combined effect that long working hours and having young children was having on some of my close friendships, so I started having a weekly early morning phone call with my best friend on the drive to work – hands-free, of course. Making time for personal relationships beyond your school will nourish you and provide the energy necessary to approach the challenges and joys of leadership afresh.

✳ Create a culture that allows your staff to have lives beyond work too

Changing her own approach to work made Allana much more aware of what she expected from those she line managed:

"You have to evolve personally because as you get older your mindset is going to change. The things that are significant for you are going to change, things in your personal life are going to change. That makes you far more reflective about how working practices are for the people who you lead. Are they getting what they need in their personal lives? Are they looking after their wellbeing? Are they managing their workload?"

I've already touched on how my own experience of having a breakdown shaped my views on the importance of wellbeing. When I returned to work, I decided that I could never get to such a low point again. Nor could I be the cause of a similar experience for anybody else. In my next role, and in later SLT positions, I ensured that I created a culture that was high achieving but sustainable. This involved small practical things – for example, I didn't send emails outside of certain hours or request unnecessarily fast turnarounds – as well as a shift in attitude.

✳ Find what brings you joy beyond your job and spend time doing it

Allana is absolutely passionate about growing other leaders and creating networks. The reasons stem from her own moral purpose:

"I want every child to have the opportunity for an education like the one my son has had, but I can't do that by myself because I can only affect one school, maybe influence three schools at most. I want a network of people who have that same moral purpose, who understand why that purpose is so important for every child. You're only going to get that if you grow other leaders. If I can produce six middle leaders and five assistant heads, and help them get to where they need to be and get them to the next step and give them an insight into the interviews and into how to deal with people, then that makes the profession better. I lead with the intention that the people I lead are going to flourish and perhaps end up in a better position than I did when I went through the whole process."

This sense of moral purpose has led Allana to speak at events around the country and to train aspiring and current leaders in her spare time. It led her to co-found a national grass-roots movement, BAMEed, encouraging better representation of people from Black, Asian and ethnic minority backgrounds in school leadership.[7] Allana has turned her own experiences into learning points for others:

"I've now got confidence from my journey and from having to struggle and be resilient. Now I'd like to support others so they don't have to go through as much as I did, in order for them to make the few steps of progress that I have."

Decide what works for you and make time for it. If you don't know what does, then try different activities until one really resonates. I've taken classes in roller skating, salsa dancing and clay modelling but photography and the other storytelling skills I've learnt as a result are what have really stuck for me.

Parting words

Allana was very clear about the importance of leaders being fully rounded human beings, defined by more than their job title:

"Within leadership you need to remember that you are a human first. Use every opportunity in your personal and your professional life and use those to give you the keys and indicators for leadership."

---

7 See https://www.bameednetwork.com/.

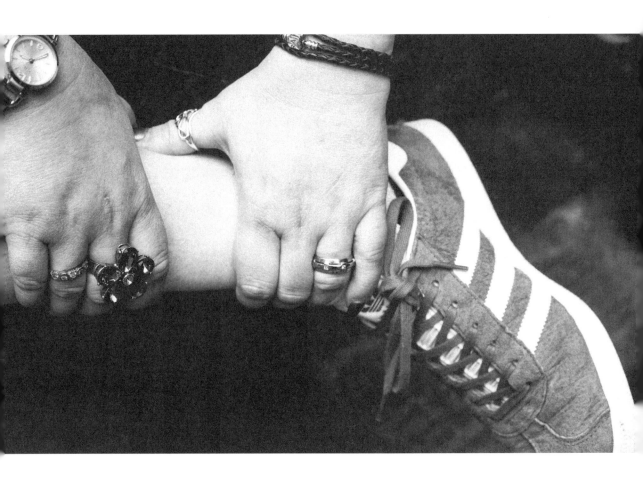

CHAPTER 8

I have experienced depression – Keziah's story

"I find it very difficult to be open emotionally, full stop. It's not about my credibility. Often my husband and closest friends don't know when I'm in the middle of a bad time."

You

* You are competent. More than that, you are highly skilled. You are respected.

* You are good at your job. You know this objectively; there is evidence.

* People look up to you. They think you have it all together.

* You do. Mostly.

* What they don't know is that you have a secret.

* You have lost all interest in the things you usually love. Music brings you no joy. Your hobbies seem pointless.

* There are times when you are so filled with self-loathing that you cannot get out of bed.

* Sometimes, you drive into work and find yourself crying for no reason at all. All you know is you feel overwhelmed with despair.

* You really ought to be happy. From the outside everybody thinks things are going well for you. Why do you feel this way?

* You wonder what is wrong with you. Then you realise. You are depressed.

* But nobody really seems to notice. Perhaps you feel numb inside but you can still function at a pretty decent level in your job, so nobody is really aware. Maybe people who know you well think you are a little quieter than usual, but that's about it.

* Maybe, after many weeks or months, you've seen your doctor and the antidepressants she prescribed are helping you deal with things day to day. Or perhaps things are actually starting to take their toll a bit and you aren't sure how much longer you can keep up the pretence.

* You use all of your energy to act normal and interact at work. When you go home there is nothing left.

＊ You come in and go straight to bed. Sometimes you can sleep for hours on end and still feel shattered. Other times you are exhausted but cannot fall asleep.

＊ It's increasingly hard to concentrate. Meetings go by and you realise you've not really taken anything in.

＊ Leaders are supposed to be strong. This is a sign of weakness. If people find out they may question whether you can do the job. You worry that some people may use this against you.

＊ You are not your depression. Despite your fears, you can still be respected. You can still have a positive impact on others.[1] Admitting your humanity will make you stronger.

If you are depressed, or have experienced depression, you won't be alone in your school community, nor among your peers, friends or family. Having more people in positions of authority who are honest about this will make it easier for others in the future. There is an idea that leaders must be strong and invulnerable. It's known that teaching is a stressful profession, and leaders are used to providing support and reassurance for staff in difficulty. Figures about the state of teachers' mental health make for sobering reading. Research undertaken by teaching unions has suggested that 1 in 10 teachers are taking antidepressants.[2] Data from the Office for National Statistics reveals that the suicide rate for primary school teachers is almost double the national average.[3] School leaders clearly have a

---

1 The Time to Change campaign reports that stigma and discrimination related to mental ill health can prevent people from seeking help. However, they have created a national movement to change conversations around mental health – and stories like mine, Keziah's and possibly yours can help. See https://www.time-to-change.org.uk/why-attitudes-mental-health-matter.

2 NASWUT research quoted in Rachael Pells, One in Ten Teachers Taking Antidepressants to Cope with Work Stresses, *The Independent* (16 April 2017). Available at: https://www.independent.co.uk/news/education/education-news/teachers-antidepressants-stress-workload-suicidal-one-in-ten-nasuwt-a7684466.html.

3 Reported in May Bulman, Primary School Teachers' Suicide Rate Nearly Double National Average, Figures Reveal, *The Independent* (17 March 2017). Available at: https://www.independent.co.uk/news/uk/home-news/primary-school-teachers-suicide-rate-double-national-average-uk-figures-a7635846.html.

duty to support staff in crisis, however, less thought is given to those leaders who may be having a hard time themselves.[4] There is a stigma around mental health issues even though it is estimated that around 1 in 4 people will experience them each year in the UK.[5] We all know that mental ill health is a problem but we're seemingly reluctant to admit to experiencing it, and this is especially the case with school leaders.

Me

This chapter started as an idea for a blog post which I was never brave enough to publish. The draft is still on my computer. At that point, I had not yet been officially open about my own periodic issues with depression in a professional context, beyond confiding in one or two people, and it felt exposing to label myself in something that was linked to my work as a school leader. I worried that admitting that I had experienced depression might affect my future employment chances.

I hadn't originally intended to include a chapter about mental health in this book, but when I had almost finished my first draft I read a chapter in *Tools of Titans* by the entrepreneur Tim Ferriss called "Some practical thoughts on suicide".[6] He spoke about his own mental health issues and I realised that if I had read an account like the one I have gone on to write earlier in my career, it would have really helped me. I was being a coward by not sharing this in writing and potentially helping somebody else.

Everyone has bad times, even accomplished people. Depression has been a periodic feature of my life since I was in sixth form. Almost all of the notes from certain courses during my second year of university are in my friend Sami's

---

4 For anyone who needs help, the Education Support Partnership offers a 24/7 free telephone counselling service for teachers. See https://www.educationsupportpartnership.org.uk/helping-you/telephone-support-counselling.

5 See https://www.time-to-change.org.uk/about-mental-health.

6 Tim Ferriss, *Tools of Titans: The Tactics, Routines, and Habits of Billionaires, Icons, and World-Class Performers* (London: Vermilion, 2016).

handwriting because I was suicidal for long stretches of time and did not attend lectures as I was unable to concentrate. For at least the first seven years of my teaching career I kept my recurrent depression a secret. When it became unmanageable and I had to take an occasional sick day, I never said the real reason. I have achieved many of my personal and professional goals both within and outside of depressive periods. I've occasionally had to access professional help in the form of counselling or antidepressants but with experience and time I've learnt how to effectively identify upcoming depressive episodes and manage my mental health without these things. In the resources section at the end of the book, I've listed a few blog posts in which I outline some of these ideas. It's really important to note that these are just things that I've found work for me; please seek appropriate medical advice if you think you need it. Experiencing depression has made me more empathetic and appreciative of difficulties that otherwise very effective staff may have personally from time to time. It's probably made me more approachable.

We've already indirectly encountered the issue of mental health several times in these interviews. Leah and Ben, who you met in Chapters 1 and 2, each explained how specific circumstances, related to their experience of leadership at a particular time, negatively affected their mental health. Scarlet, who you will meet in the following chapter, has a similar story to tell. Once the situation changed, their mental health improved, but they had to have the realisation that the situation was unsustainable. Allana's story, in Chapter 7, shows how important a healthy work–life balance is as a preventative measure. For many people, this will be enough to maintain their sense of wellbeing. However, for some, adjusting work–life balance may not help. For some, possibly for you, circumstantial changes are not enough and you may be living with a mental illness or encountering a period of significant mental ill health. If this is the case, well-meaning advice designed to maintain everyday wellbeing may actually make you feel worse at times. You are following it but you still feel crap. Your mood isn't lifting and it may feel like more evidence of your worthlessness.

Keziah

While it took me a long time to work up the bravery to share my experience, one person who has always been open about theirs is Keziah, who is currently a head teacher at a comprehensive secondary school in the Midlands. For that aborted blog post, I had the idea of approaching a number of senior leaders in my personal network, who I respected and knew had also experienced episodes of mental ill health. Keziah was the only person who replied to my email asking them to share their experiences.

Keziah has taught English for over two decades, beginning her career in the West Midlands. She has also led an all-through comprehensive school in the south-west of England. She was the first in her family to go to university and credits her own independent and self-sufficient outlook to her unusual childhood, part of which was spent living on a communal farm. "My family all decided to move in together in the mid-seventies. There were 16 of us living in a house," she told me. When I visited her home for our interview I was inspected by the various cats belonging to her family, and they also have an energetic hamster. When asked how her students would describe her, Keziah said, "approachable, funny and relatable" and as I watched her one Friday afternoon handing out lollipops at the end of school while talking to her departing students about their upcoming weekends I could see why.

I'm not and never have been a head teacher. I have no idea how it must be to experience or admit to depression, current or past, as the person who is ultimately accountable for everything that happens in a school. Although mental health problems are common, it's rare for people in positions of authority, like school leaders, to be honest and open about having experienced them during their careers.

Keziah outlines a period in her life as a school leader when she found it difficult to cope mentally, which affected how she felt about work but wasn't caused by it. She had just been made an acting assistant head teacher for the first time, after being at the school for six years, the latter of which were spent as a successful head of English. We join Keziah's story at a time when she was "very comfortable" and happy at her school and was trying to start a family:

"I'd always wanted to be a parent. I had some fertility issues, the specialist had told us not to bother trying for a baby any more. They weren't going to put us onto the NHS IVF list because I was too old and it just wasn't going to happen. We were three-quarters of the way through the adoption process, being assessed, then, weirdly, I got pregnant. I thought I'd be quite good at parenthood, but it turned out I was rubbish. I had postnatal depression. It just wasn't the way that it was going to go in my head. I'd never expected to be pregnant and I'd had a couple of miscarriages beforehand so I pretty much spent every day anxious and worried. When the baby turned up alive it was a hell of a shock, I don't think we'd realistically planned for it. So we hadn't built the buggy, we hadn't got any bottles or anything like that. We just weren't prepared for a real-life little human being in the house.

"When I had the baby I really struggled. While I was acting as assistant head teacher, I was still pretty much the incumbent head of English. When I was off on maternity leave they made the acting head of English permanent. I realised I didn't have a position to go back to if I was no longer acting assistant head teacher. So it was like, 'Shit, I don't have a job.' They were in no rush to make me permanent. I was dealing with postnatal depression, the impact on my relationship and having a baby without any family around. I was constantly feeling foggy and anxious and not enjoying anything. All the happiness went out of my life, there was no respite from it. Work was respite from home but then when work wasn't going that well either … I was really not in a happy place."

Added to the significant changes in her personal life, and dealing with the effects of postnatal depression, Keziah was also facing changes at work. Over a fairly short period of time, the stability that she had been used to changed. The head teacher who promoted her to the SLT left, as did a deputy head teacher, while another of her SLT colleagues went on maternity leave:

"The leadership team all vanished pretty much overnight. It was me and another assistant head teacher running the school. There wasn't any time

to get anybody else in. We did a really good job. We enjoyed it and it was fantastic working together. We had a couple of people join the team. Then a new permanent head teacher came in. The person who had been off on maternity leave was clearly going to be made a deputy and the person who had been the acting head was clearly going to be made a deputy. I was going to stay where I was and be an assistant head. I felt really aggrieved."

Everything suddenly started to seem too much:

"I think I'd been in a position where, just beforehand, I felt good. I'd just been married, I was earning a fairly reasonable sum of money, really enjoying being at work and doing really well and then, within about a year, I was out of control of everything. I had no handle on anything. I had no control. I couldn't control the child. I couldn't control how I felt about the child. I couldn't control how I felt about work. I had no emotional support for that."

Keziah felt a sense of shame about being unable to cope and kept her feelings to herself because of what she expected others' perceptions to be:

"I had fears around being open because people were already judging me for coming back to work five months after giving birth and they were suggesting that women often 're-evaluated their career ambitions' after a baby. I also feared that I was making poor decisions as a woman and as a mother and that therefore I was getting what I deserved. My friends weren't terribly supportive because they weren't in the same position as me. A lot of those friendships just broke down. Five years later when they had kids they were like, 'I understand. I understand now.' I eventually told the new head teacher, who was a man, that I had postnatal depression and he said, 'Well that's pretty obvious', but wasn't much help. I've not had an episode as bad as that since, but I do still experience some difficulties with mental health from time to time. I find it very difficult to be open emotionally, full stop. It's not about my credibility. Often my husband and closest friends don't know when I'm in the middle of a bad time."

Keziah feels that there are still barriers to head teachers and other school leaders being honest about their mental health. She feels that negative stereotypes come from a variety of sources but she urges school leaders not to hide:

"There is a stereotype that a school leader, particularly a head teacher, should have gravitas and they should have a natural authority. I've heard that said by members of staff, by people who are on governing bodies, by HR professionals, by other head teachers. That's why they say it's lonely at the top. If you break that perception with the reality that, actually, sometimes mental illness certainly gets in the way of gravitas, then that changes the narrative and you're no longer on a pedestal. People have said to me that they want a head teacher who looks like they're not going to take any shit from anybody. In terms of people giving me feedback on my leadership, that lack of gravitas is occasionally commented on, as is my personality, but even if I hadn't struggled with mental health issues in the past, I was never going to be that person. You have to know who you are, you have to be confident, you have to be happy in being the best leader you can be. I think if you are putting it on and pretending, it's never going to sound very authentic. You're never going to believe it and nobody's going to believe in you."

Keziah's earlier period of depression was linked to feeling a lack of control over various aspects of her life and I know that I have felt similar during my most severe periods of depression. She makes clear links to the current situation for school leaders and what she feels head teachers are and are not able to control:

"There are things that now that I'm a head I feel I can control and can manage and there are things that are beyond my control. Weirdly for me, the things I can control are all the shit that is external to my school. The government, the Department for Education and Ofsted and all that kind of stuff. I can be like an umbrella and I can deflect it and protect my staff. The things that I can't control, that I get very anxious over are, I suppose, some of the contextual factors that affect the children's progress, especially in a school

serving historically deprived areas, these are massive and we should be able to compensate for that. I'm trying to find a way to compensate for that while having to cut half-a-million pounds off the school budget."[7]

Despite the pressures and occasional frustrations, Keziah is passionate about and loves being a head teacher, as is clear throughout our discussion. Ultimately, Keziah has decided that perfection is not necessary and that you can do your job well without having to be a superhuman:

"It's okay to make mistakes, it's okay to worry at times and be anxious. There are times when you just have to act appropriately and project those leadership behaviours. So, if GCSE results next week are absolutely bloody awful, then people will look to me for how to respond to that and I understand that. I'm not going to lie in the corner and cry. 'Where's the head? Oh, she's rocking herself to sleep!' By being appropriately vulnerable I hope I'll also make headship more appealing. It's bloody exhausting, but awesome. Hopefully staff will start to think, 'I can be myself and not know all the answers to everything and still do that job.'"

What can we learn from Keziah's story?

* You don't need to be a superhero

As a school leader it can feel like failure to admit any flaws. Staff may expect you to know all the answers and you sometimes might have to be the person who is there to support them or for them to project their emotions onto. People are sometimes surprised that leaders have feelings too. Keziah reminds us:

---

7   Research from the Education Policy Institute found that, "At national level, secondary schools with larger proportions (over 30 per cent) of FSM pupils are set to lose funding (around £4.0m in total)". See Natalie Perera, Jon Andrews and Peter Sellen, *The Implications of the National Funding Formula for Schools* (London: Education Policy Institute, 2017). Available at: https://epi.org.uk/publications-and-research/implications-national-funding-formula-schools/, p. 37.

"You're human. You don't always find things easy but it is possible to put on a smile and get on with it. I have done assemblies where I have shared stories about difficult events but I personally find this easier with a time lag – at the time it is too raw."

One of the first ever assemblies I ran as an assistant head in a new school was about gratitude, as I mentioned briefly in Chapter 3. As the kids entered to "Happy" by Pharrell Williams, they saw me dancing and singing along. Obviously the students were a bit confused at first. In the main part of the assembly, I revealed the science around gratitude and explained my own struggles with depression before reading a few entries from my old gratitude journal aloud. Five years later I was teaching GCSE maths to some Year 11 students who had been sitting in that assembly as fresh-faced Year 7s. Completely out of the blue, they told me that that assembly had stuck with them and they could still remember the message. Sometimes sharing something of ourselves with the students, in the right context, can be very powerful.

✳ Make sure you confide in the right people

Over the past fourteen years I have taught in a number of schools with hundreds of staff and it's telling that I've only spoken to two of my colleagues explicitly about my depression. Keziah also explains the importance of choosing the right people to confide in. "I confided personal stuff to people who gossiped and it just killed me off." Luckily, as her career has progressed, Keziah has found that there are people she can share difficulties with:

"People say that headship is the loneliest job in the school. Actually, no. It is if you make it so. It is if you keep yourself cut off. I wouldn't sit down with my assistant head and say, 'You know what, I'm finding it really difficult at the moment.' But I can with my chair of governors and a couple of other people. There are a couple of other heads that are really good to talk to. As long as you're there for them as well, or else it's very selfish, isn't it?"

✳ Take time when you need it, even a small amount can help

During our interview, Keziah outlined the importance of the relationships she had with her PA, chair of governors and senior team. She describes one episode in which these relationships were invaluable after a major incident at her school, which was compounded by negative comments from parents on social media:

> "I just went up the stairs and said to my PA, Jo, 'I need five minutes.' I went into my office and I shut the door and I sat there and dealt with my emotions. I was meant to be having a meeting with a colleague, and Jo was like, 'You can't go in there at the moment.' Eventually he came up. I said, 'I needed five minutes to myself. It just reached peak stress, peak anxiety.' He said, 'I'm so glad that I saw you doing that, because I know that it's okay when I need to.' The whole staff, each individual person, was trying to hold themselves together for everybody else and actually, although I shouldn't have my five minutes in the middle of the dining hall, it's okay for me to need to go into my office and shut the door and just put myself back together again."

✳ Openness builds more openness

I know of at least four senior leaders in my close professional network who have experienced depression of some type. Once I became more open about my experience, I was comfortable mentioning it when doing workshops and speeches, which meant many others told me about their own experiences. Keziah has found this too, "I do now speak more openly. I have chatted to colleagues at work about the postnatal depression, because it is so common."

✳ Learn to manage your emotions

Early in my career I had no way of dealing with stress. My temper was explosive and although I was under pressure, severely depressed and lacking sleep I'm still ashamed of my reaction to certain events. Keziah outlines the danger of keeping emotional difficulties hidden but also explains that our own issues are not an excuse to react disproportionally to others, especially if we are in a leadership position:

> "When I was a deputy, I worked with a head teacher who had no way of managing his emotions. I had seen him go absolutely mental in front of parents. He scared people. He exploded several times when it was just me and him. He exploded at another member of staff in a room full of other people. I don't think I've ever done that. I think people can tell that I'm slightly grumpy but I won't lose my temper in front of them."

When I was relatively new to teaching, a fight broke out, seemingly from nowhere, in one of my lessons. My first thought was to separate those fighting. There was another teacher, who at the time was more senior than me, in the classroom opposite. I asked if she could quickly take one of the students away. For whatever reason, she said no and to say I was irritated by this would be an understatement. I went ballistic. It probably didn't help that I'd been experiencing severe insomnia for many weeks due to my depression, but nobody knew about that. I completely lost my temper and remember the question "What's the point of you?" and a few expletives leaving my mouth and flying in her general direction. Obviously the fighting kids stopped and all eyes were now on me, wide as saucers. I calmly returned to teaching and we finished the lesson. By lunchtime it was all around the school that, "Ms Small hit Ms Kahlid, I saw it with my own two eyes."[8] Like Keziah's former head teacher, I had no way to manage my emotions. This meant that the incident became about my reaction rather than about an experienced member of staff failing to support a new teacher. Don't let this happen to you. I later found supportive colleagues in my department who helped me manage personal time-outs – usually only a minute or so was effective – from heightened situations when I was sleep deprived.

---

8   Not her real name. There was in fact around 5 to 10 metres of space between us at all times during the exchange but teenagers won't always let facts get in the way of a good story.

* Find a way to support others who are having a tough time

Leaders are human but we are also paid to take responsibility. People look to us in a variety of ways and there is nuance in knowing when to be open and how to deal with emotions or mental health difficulties while at work. Keziah shared an episode in which she supported members of her SLT to deal with a tragic school event:

> *"We had a child die. If that wasn't hard enough for everyone to deal with there was all this fallout afterwards, things on social media and accusations from parents. Some of my senior team found it very, very difficult, two of them in particular. I said, 'I need you to take some time off to deal with this.' They were refusing. Ultimately, one of them came up with an idea. They came in late one day so they could watch a really early British Lions rugby match together. They had that time off together but they weren't sitting at home thinking about stuff and grieving. Then they came in and it gave them a little bit of a kick up the arse."*

* Blame is pointless and adds to poor mental health for staff

Keziah was critical of particular school cultures that can be created by leadership teams as a result of perceived hyperaccountability:

> *"Where there is a high blame culture, people are just far more stressed out. Actually, I like to think my leadership is quite low blame; low threat, high challenge. Because otherwise you burn people out and make them ill. Be kind to yourself, for a start. It's really easy to beat yourself up."*

I honestly believe that if we want to create an environment where staff can do their best for our students then we need to see mistakes as a way to learn and do better rather than as irredeemable or career-ending. Aren't we always trying to get students to embrace the value of mistakes? We also need to take a look at the accountability culture. My own work-related breakdown happened partly because, in addition to carrying out my role, I had to spend a lot of time justifying what I was doing and proving that I was doing what I said I would via countless meetings, forms and emails. This added huge swathes to my workload and eventually became unsustainable.

As a senior leader I didn't want to repeat the mistakes of people I'd been managed by. I looked for opportunities to remove all unnecessary or onerous tasks that had no obvious impact on students' leaning and decided that trust was a great way to reduce stress and anxiety for staff. Blame is a waste of time. I've found that it's much better to accept that something hasn't worked and then to see what can be learnt from the experience to help decide what can be changed or improved for next time. It's a cop out for leadership teams to blame Ofsted, it's up to you to determine the working culture in your own school. Karen's story, in Chapter 6, was a powerful lesson about healthy working culture. In the next chapter, Scarlet's experiences of a toxic culture provide a stark contrast.

Parting words

While Keziah's mental health issues were not initially triggered by work, she was clear that mental health needs to be addressed across the education sector if we are to retain teachers:

> "If we're going to deal with the recruitment and retention problem, we need to help educators deal with their mental health better. Particularly stress levels, anxiety levels and coping with feelings of failure. I don't think the English stiff upper lip way of doing stuff is the way to do that. You need to give people an outlet so they can say, 'You know what? I'm finding it really difficult at the moment.'"

Finally, I asked her how she felt about herself as a leader, particularly one who doesn't conform to the traditional stereotype:

> "Leadership is about making things better for others. If you genuinely want to make things better for other people and you think you can make that happen,

then it's worth doing it. You don't have to fit into a type of box. I'm not sure if I'd get my tattoos out, put my nose stud in and go in to school with pink hair, there are some compromises that you have to make. But you can be different. We just need more leaders who genuinely want to make a difference."[9]

---

9   Keziah has written about what she calls punk leaders, who fit the description she gives. Keziah Featherstone, Punk Leadership Means Daring to Think Outside the System, *Schools Week* (23 June 2018). Available at: https://schoolsweek.co.uk/punk-leadership-means-daring-to-think-outside-the-system/.

CHAPTER 9

I don't want to lead any more – Scarlet's story

"There was a culture of fear, if I'm honest, and I was scared too. You know what, I think the leaders were all scared."

You

∗ You've worked hard to get to this point. You're in a senior leadership position. You wanted to make a difference, have a wider impact, but now you are questioning yourself.

∗ When you go to bed you can't sleep. When nobody is around and it's quiet you think to yourself, "I don't think this is right for me any more."

∗ You've had enough. The position. The title. The expectations. Maybe even teaching itself.

∗ But leaders aren't supposed to quit. They aren't supposed to resign. Unless they are asked to, or forced to.

∗ So many people would like to be in a position like yours. You thought you wanted a position like yours. You wanted to be part of the solution.

∗ You don't want to let people down. Your family, yourself.

∗ And if you quit … then what?

The statistics certainly confirm that you are not the only person to have thought about leaving the profession. Data from the National Foundation for Educational Research (NFER) showed that 20% of teachers surveyed were considering leaving within the next year.[1] Whatever you decide, do not feel ashamed. Read on and realise that you do have choices and that nothing is final or fixed. Make a decision, act on it and see how it goes. Just don't leave things as they are if they are not right for you.

It may seem odd to conclude a book about leadership with a chapter aimed at people who no longer want to lead, but the truth is that this is a reality for some and these decisions are not to be made lightly. Perhaps you'll realise that, actually,

---

1   Jack Worth, Susan Bamford and Ben Durbin (2015). *Should I Stay or Should I Go? NFER Analysis of Teachers Joining and Leaving the Profession* (Slough: NFER, 2015). Available at: https://www.nfer.ac.uk/publications/LFSA01/LFSA01.pdf, pp. 6–7.

you really do want to stay. You may realise that your current school is the place for you but that you need to talk to your boss about specific issues that have been affecting your enjoyment of the role. Or you may realise that leadership is right for you but your current school isn't.

Me

When I was an assistant head teacher I realised that the job really wasn't working for me any more. I wish I could tell you some dramatic reason why or relate a particular incident that made me feel that way, but the truth is that there wasn't one. It had been a creeping feeling. I felt like I wasn't having the impact I wanted to and that I needed a change. I sat mutely in meetings that I had previously been keen to contribute to, waiting for them to end. They felt pointless to me, with little relation to why I'd originally gone into teaching. I did the obvious and started applying for promotions in other schools, but when I paid attention to myself I realised I had no real enthusiasm for the roles that I was applying for. It dawned on me that I didn't actually want to be a senior leader any more. In some ways I had returned to how I initially felt at the very start of my career, when, as a young maths teacher, I had looked at the positions ahead of me on the ladder and found them unappealing. So now what? I would have to think.

Scarlet

Scarlet currently teaches English in a secondary school in the east of England. She has been teaching for almost two decades and during that time has worked in the north-west and south of England, in London and in northern France. Scarlet has taught in a variety of schools serving economically disadvantaged communities and says, "I genuinely believe that education can change a kid's life."

She describes herself as, "the sort of child who would make her little sister put on different voices and answer the register with her line of toys at the age of about 6 or 7". Scarlet always knew she wanted to be a teacher, describing the only choice she had to make about her career as, "Do I teach English or do I teach art?" The walls of her home are decorated with large, bold, painted portraits, so her love of art has clearly remained even though she chose English.

When I first met Scarlet she was an assistant head teacher but her route to senior leadership hadn't been planned. She became an AST because she was passionate about teaching, learning and training especially, "working with NQTs and sharing the buzz that they still have". Then she took a promotion at a different school and became part of the SLT. To Scarlet, school leadership is, "The most important job in the world, other than being a classroom teacher, and really bloody hard to do well."

Scarlet is from a close-knit family and grew up just outside London. When I asked her to describe her perfect Sunday afternoon she said, "It would be with my sister and nieces reading books and eating ice cream."

Scarlet and I met at the first ever WomenEd conference, where I was giving a talk about my journey to authentic leadership. By coincidence, we discovered that she lived very close to where I taught at the time. Scarlet had got together with a small group of other female senior leaders and decided that there needed to be a network to support and encourage women to apply for leadership roles in education, where they were underrepresented. They got sponsorship and created a national grass-roots movement, but that's a story for another time. It's somewhat ironic that about a year after meeting at a leadership conference both of us voluntarily resigned from our school leadership roles. Scarlet's reasons were different to mine but the feelings of denial, shame and loss of identity were the same.

Scarlet had always wanted to teach, as she explained to me during our interview. There had never been a plan B. She loved teaching English and became an AST so that she could take on a classroom-based leadership role while developing other English teachers. About a decade into her career, Scarlet found herself at a crossroads:

> "I did the AST route and after a while I found myself a bit bored. I was developing other staff but felt like was I stagnating in my own practice and not really developing professionally. I was headhunted and asked to work

in a school as part of their SLT. I thought, 'Why not? Let's give it a go.' It seemed like a great opportunity."

Scarlet's new role involved improving teaching and learning across the school, as well as enabling teachers to develop in their professional practice. But she soon realised that her own views were fundamentally at odds with what she was expected to implement as a senior leader:

"I believed that there was more than one way to ensure good teaching across the school but my voice wasn't listened to. Everybody had to do everything in the same way. That's what had always been done in that school. It can have benefits. I think when you're telling all teachers that you need to start a lesson in this way, then you do x, then you do extended writing for half an hour, then you do y, every single lesson of every single day, you are pulling up the teachers who need that additional help, support and structure but you're also in serious risk of restricting and handcuffing the teachers who can make lessons mind-blowing and phenomenal, the kind of lessons that kids remember forever.

"I very quickly found myself extremely disheartened and it didn't take me long to realise that I just couldn't align my views on education with the ethos of the school. I had no autonomy. I felt extremely oppressed by the way in which I had to teach. My biggest issue was the way teachers were treated. I was working with a lot of NQTs, a lot of Teach First trainees who were struggling with the workload. I had so many NQTs coming to me crying and the message from above was, 'That's what teaching's like, that's the message you need to give them.' I didn't believe that teaching had to be like that. The exam results were great but I couldn't buy into the vision."

Scarlet knew that her values were at odds with the school but she continued to work through it. She had been committed to teaching for her entire working life and had faced many challenges in her career but one day she had a feeling that she had never experienced before:

"I didn't realise straight away, but disillusionment sort of crept up on me. I was walking to school from the station and I just thought, 'I don't want to go to work.' Sure, I've often thought, 'Oh I can't believe the alarm's gone off. How's my sleep over already?' But in all my years of teaching I've never thought, 'I don't want to go to work today. I don't want to see those teachers. I don't want to see my line manager. I don't believe what they believe. I don't think they are going about education in the right way.'"

Scarlet was able to empathise with teachers' concerns around workload because as well as being an assistant head teacher she still had a fairly sizeable number of lessons to teach herself. As part of a hard-working English department she knew she had to set a good example but her own health was starting to suffer:

"I was unwell and part of that was because of the unhappiness that I was feeling. I was working long hours to keep on top of everything and not be the one who let the team down. I remember feeling like I was unravelling just before I quit. I said to my line manager, 'I'm working 7 a.m. to 7 p.m., sometimes 8 p.m., then I'm travelling an hour either end of that. I have no life. I don't get a minute in the day to mark these books. I've got all these books to mark. I can't possibly do it.' The advice I was given? 'Well, school's open on Saturday, you can come in and mark then. Or you can bring in a suitcase and take all your books home in that.' And I laughed and I said, 'You are joking, right?' I got a blank-faced 'No.' And I just thought, 'I'm done.'"

As we learnt from Allana in Chapter 7, one event can trigger the realisation that you have to change a situation that has been a problem for some time. This particular conversation was that moment for Scarlet but she still had some reluctance to leave. Her self-worth as a human being was very closely intertwined with her professional identity, as is the case for many of us:

"I didn't want to fail. I couldn't bring myself to quit. I couldn't bring myself to say that my role wasn't working. I thought, 'What am I going to do? If I don't

believe that education is fundamentally good for staff and children, what do I believe and who am I?' I was ill and stressed and panicky and basically found myself a sobbing wreck on my mum and dad's sofa. They'd seen me wanting to be a teacher since the age of six, they knew there hadn't been another plan. I said to them, 'I don't believe in education. I think it's corrupt. I think it's wrong. I think it's damaging children. I think it's damaging teachers. No wonder all these teachers are leaving.' They obviously gasped and said, 'Oh my goodness, what's going on here?' In the end my mum and dad made me type my resignation. It was probably the hardest decision of my career because I'm not one who gives up. My mum went and posted it while I sat nervously on the sofa with my dad, who was trying to inspire me by making me watch a movie!

"I then had a couple of months where I worked out what I was going to do. Other senior leaders I spoke to, in my wider network, said, 'It sounds like you've done the right thing, just take some time, decide what you want to do. If you don't want to teach any more, that's a real shame but it might become clear what you do want to do in the next month.'"

While she was working out her next step, Scarlet had a conversation with a former colleague who was working with a charity in refugee camps in Europe. This discussion took her career in an unexpected direction:

"He said, 'If you've got time on your hands then come out here and work with the children in the camps. It might make you see education from a different viewpoint. It might make you stop sulking and being a mardy cow,' which was a fair point. In those refugee camps I met teachers who were teaching with nothing, who were teaching out of love and passion, not because of what Ofsted might say and not because of what a leader might come and tell you off for. They were there with the bare minimum, doing what they thought was the best for those children. It did give me a reality check and remind me why I wanted to be a teacher in the first place. It's about teachers and humans and humanity as well as empowering children and providing them with an education."

Scarlet's time teaching in Europe provided enough space and distance to reconnect her with the younger version of herself who had pretended to be the teacher of her sister and teddy bears:

"I started missing being part of a school community. I also got to the point where my mortgage payment was looming and I realised I was running low on funds. There were a range of reasons why, but I found myself back part-time in a school fifteen minutes up the road, just not as a senior leader. I rediscovered my love of teaching. At first I worked there for three days a week and continued to do the charity work for two days a week, but I went from part-time back to full-time this year. I'm a specialist leader in education (SLE) and I am doing some work leading on CPD. In the school that I'm in at the moment, they believe in trust and honesty, so ethos-wise I can align myself. Things are so much better now."

What can we learn from Scarlet's story?

* Leaving leadership is not the first option for every disagreement

Part of leadership is knowing when to compromise. You won't agree with everything that happens in your school. As Scarlet says, "As a leader you have to compromise at times. I think you need to know when you are right and fight that as far as you possibly can." Sometimes fighting isn't needed. Leadership isn't just about having all the best ideas and imposing them on people. When I first became a leader, I was very insistent on things being done in particular ways – for instance, as a head of department I became convinced that teachers should not be using textbooks as that is what made some students declare that they hate maths and find it boring. Then I realised that the method isn't necessarily that important; a boring ineffective lesson is a boring ineffective lesson with or without textbooks. Outcome is more important, and as I got better at managing people and drawing out their strengths, I've definitely come round to Scarlet's way of thinking:

"I also think you need to know sometimes that there's more than one way to do it and someone else might have greater expertise or greater experience or a better idea and I think you need the humility to accept that."

✳ Know when it is definitely time to leave

Sometimes you may reach a point where you have made reasonable compromises, raised concerns with colleagues or changed your working practices but it still isn't enough. Scarlet offered some clear pointers about how to judge when your particular role at your particular school really isn't right for you:

"Run for the hills when your health or relationships are being damaged. I don't think any school leader or teacher is going to lie on their deathbed and think, 'Oh, if only I'd done a bit more work on the school improvement plan' or 'If only I'd spent a little bit longer on that one performance management observation.' I think that when health and relationships are being impacted to a point where you're not seeing friends, you're not seeing family, you're unwell, you have to make a change. You have tried to compromise but cannot align yourself to the culture or the ethos and your moral compass is screaming at you every morning, 'This is wrong. This is wrong.' I think life's too short to be dragging yourself into a job where you know that you're not going to make a difference because no one will listen or no one will value your view."

✳ Fear is crippling sections of our education system

Scarlet acknowledged that her school got very good results but that it was at what she felt was too high a price. There is a problem with our current educational system. Extremely high accountability and what feels like no room for failure is creating a climate of unhealthy fear and competition for school leaders. This disproportionately affects schools serving disadvantaged areas; in fact, schools in poor areas are five times more likely to be given the lowest Ofsted ratings:[2]

---

2   John Roberts, Is Ofsted Fit to Judge Deprived Schools?, *TES* (16 June 2018). Available at: https://www.tes.com/news/ofsted-fit-judge-deprived-schools.

"There was a culture of fear, if I'm honest, and I was scared too. You know what, I think the leaders were all scared. It was very much this fear being filtered down. Fear of results going down, of trying anything new. It was part of a chain so there was always worry around which school would be the first to fall from Ofsted's 'outstanding' to just 'good'. There's this sort of incredible pressure, that's something that some MATs have built their success on because no one wants to be that first school who drops down or who is put into special measures."

This pressure created the conditions that made Scarlet want to leave her job and also could be part of the reason why 3 out of 10 new school leaders resign within the first five years.[3] Unreasonable accountability around exam results, which impact Ofsted ratings, also lead to dedicated head teachers being asked to leave.[4] Even just in my own professional network I know of four head teachers who were either sacked or asked to resign. I agree with accountability but not as it is: something in our current system needs to change. Ultimately this instability will affect children's educations.

✳ Understand who you are and what you believe in

Scarlet and I are in agreement that even wonderful schools are not utopias:

"There is no such thing as a perfect school. I'm not going to suggest jumping out of a school because you are a little fed up with a particular policy. I walked because it was not right for me. My moral compass was screaming at me on a daily basis."

---

3   Eleanor Busby, Three in 10 New School Leaders Quit in the First Five Years, Figures Reveal, *The Independent* (5 May 2018). Available at: https://www.independent.co.uk/news/education/education-news/school-leaders-headteachers-quit-teacher-retention-crisis-angela-rayner-labour-naht-a8337661.html.

4   Anonymous, 'Sacked from the School I Loved': A Headteacher's Story, *The Guardian* (24 October 2017). Available at: https://www.theguardian.com/education/2017/oct/24/sacked-school-headteacher-alevel-results.

Before you make major decisions about your career you have to understand what matters to you, who you are, what your beliefs are and if they've changed since you've started. Scarlet realised that she had to take time out to think. In some ways she's still trying to follow the advice given by a former boss, "You just need to work out what a Scarlet is." She reflected:

> "I don't know. A Scarlet is a gobby girl who admits when she's wrong but who inherently believes that kindness and education are something that every child is and should be entitled to."

Like Scarlet, I needed time to work out what mattered to me and what I wanted. One day I sat down and wrote a brief list of priorities, outlining what I believe in, how I want my life to look, the kind of work I want to do and the impact I want to have on others and on society. Doing this really helped and has made subsequent decisions easier to make. I'm a step closer to aligning myself with this list but, like Scarlet, I still feel like I'm a work in progress.

✳ Leading isn't just about a title

Scarlet has returned to working in a school full-time. She has a classroom-based role but has found different ways to influence and impact other teachers within and beyond her school:

> "I really believe you can lead in different ways. You can lead in being open and honest. I've been involved with a massive coaching network. It has been liberating that I can just go in and be a classroom teacher but at the same time, outside of school, I can do stuff like the WomenEd conference. I think my voice is still one that people see as leadership. Sometimes you can lead people and help them in their career without directly working with them."

After resigning, Scarlet blogged about her experience:

"My blog resonated with a lot of people because I was saying things that were seen as a weakness to show. Sometimes by having ups and downs, those ins and outs, you learn more. There's no harm in making mistakes. Leaders don't have to be these infallible creatures."

I was initially worried about writing a book for school leaders now that I am no longer one. A number of people in my external network told me not to worry about it. "Experience and knowledge over titles," one of them said. If leadership is about influence then I've decided to use mine to try to help others. If you are considering leaving school leadership, you can still be influential in different ways.

✳ Create a financial buffer

Often we know what we have to do but fear and our very real responsibilities and financial obligations prevent us from making a change. Scarlet mentioned in passing that she had a small amount of savings which allowed her to resign without a job lined up while she worked out her next step:

"I then had a couple of months of time to work out what I was going to do. I had the money to take a short breather."

Very soon after I interviewed Scarlet I was talking to another head teacher who mentioned that she too had an emergency fund which meant she never felt trapped in a job. I thought this sounded like a good idea but at first it seemed impossible for me. My partner and I have three young children, two of whom were in day care at the time, and I am the main breadwinner in our family. However, with careful planning, over a few years I saved up my own small buffer. You hope you'll never need it, but knowing that you have a few months of financial flexibility helps you feel less trapped in a job and able to make clear decisions that aren't based on desperation and fear.

✳ An interview isn't a one-way street

Scarlet realised fairly quickly after starting her SLT role that her ethos didn't align with the school's, but it would have saved her a lot of time and pain if she'd been able to tell this at interview. During our discussion Scarlet spoke about the need to appraise a school:

> *"Now if I was going for an interview, maybe I'd pin down the three things that I cannot compromise on. Schools often write about their philosophies and values. I think, in the future, I'd be that very annoying person in the interview asking, 'Well you say this is what you value but how? Why? If I were to walk around your school now, where would I see that actually being done? Can we go and look?' I'd ask for examples of where they have had an issue with the values and how they've resolved it, or how the values are embedded in the curriculum even. I'd be able to tell how well they know their school."*

Perhaps you'd worry that an interview panel might find questions like these annoying, but if they do then it's a great indicator that the school probably isn't for you. You may be pleasantly surprised. As an assistant head teacher, I line managed the SENCO. During an interview, a candidate asked about the school's inclusion philosophy and for examples of how we put it into practice day to day. With barely a pause, the SENCO, who was passionate about inclusion and about creating the very best learning environment for the children she was responsible for, clearly and passionately explained her educational philosophy for children with SEN. She then explained to the candidate how each member of the department specifically helped to fulfil it. It was a beautiful moment and the candidate clearly had a similar philosophy.

Parting words

You don't have to know all the answers, you just need to start asking the questions and taking small steps in the right direction for you. Scarlet's experiences since resigning her SLT post are helping her to form her own guiding principles:

> "Leadership can be like a slinky, it doesn't always have to be a straight upward trajectory. I'm slowly learning now that what I'm really passionate about is equity in education, whether it be for women leaders, whether it be for the refugee children in those camps, who are sometimes there on their own. Or indeed for the kids who've had a year of cover at the start of their GCSEs and only been picked up by a permanent teacher in Year 11."

Conclusion

"External networks are what make leaders."

Us

* We are all different.

* New leader.

* Experienced leader.

* Vocally opinionated leader.

* Quiet leader.

* We are each unexpected in our own way, in our own context.

All the leaders we have met are different and unique in their own ways, and have had a host of varying experiences that have made them the people they are, and led them to their current positions. Now is the time to reflect on what they have in common.

When I first thought of writing this book, I wanted to focus on different facets of what made me and my interviewees unexpected in our own settings. However, as I began to talk to the school leaders featured in the preceding pages, I started to notice that some themes came up again and again. This conclusion is my attempt to distil the commonalities in the experiences of these leaders. They are the lessons that particularly spoke to me and that I have found myself reflecting and acting on repeatedly since the interviews.

What can we learn from the collective experience of unexpected leaders?

* Find a community, or make your own

You may feel isolated in your school, but remember that your school isn't the world. There will be like-minded people that you can connect with in your region or further afield, either in person or virtually. Leah and Karen are friends who happen to be in education but I met my other interviewees as a result of putting myself out there and attending events that chime with my professional interests and personal beliefs.

Scarlet and Allana each co-founded their own national network as they felt that existing and established groups didn't cater for what they needed as leaders. They wanted to create opportunities for other leaders like them, and build supportive communities. Scarlet's work with WomenEd[1] is designed to connect existing and aspiring female leaders in education, and through BAMEed[2] Allana aims to improve opportunities for leaders from Black, Asian or minority ethnic backgrounds.

In *Show Your Work!*, the writer and artist Austin Kleon talks about the importance of finding or creating what he calls a "scenius", a group of peers who you can contribute ideas to and learn from.[3] This is also explored by the singer Patti Smith in *Just Kids*.[4] She describes her time living in New York at the Hotel Chelsea with the photographer Robert Mapplethorpe, slowly creating their own community of artists before they were both famous. This collaboration clearly helps to unleash creativity in the arts, and is something that we can learn from as leaders too. Allana was very clear in her view: "I think external networks are what make leaders." Her own network is what helped her bounce back and remain in school leadership after sudden redundancy.

But you don't need to start a national network. Perhaps you'll find an established organisation that represents your interests. Or perhaps you'll get involved at a regional level, like Malcolm has done. Maybe you'll go and speak at informal grass-roots events – for example, TeachMeets, which is how I met Tait. Or perhaps you'll use social media to reach out to people, which is how I met Lila. Maybe you'll contact people via Twitter or ask them to meet up for a coffee – but whatever you do, connect. Find your people.

————

1   See http://www.womened.org/.
2   See https://www.bameednetwork.com/.
3   Austin Kleon, *Show Your Work! 10 Things Nobody Told You About Getting Discovered* (New York: Workman Publishing, 2014), p. 9.
4   Patti Smith, *Just Kids* (London: Bloomsbury, 2010), pp. 100–106.

I have learnt that leaders cannot function in isolation; you need peers and mentors who you can be honest with and learn from. I realised that one of the main mistakes I made was isolating myself because of fear or embarrassment, like when I got stuck the first time I had to write the school timetable and just panicked about being unable to finish it, rather than reaching out to peers in my wider network of school leaders for help.

✳ Keep learning

Every leader I spoke to mentioned the need to be a continual learner. Some had undertaken post-graduate study at master's level or beyond, others were excited to learn about a variety of topics beyond their immediate specialism. The collective message was clear: it is important for leaders to know their stuff. For our own self-confidence but also because if others challenge us, we need to know what we are talking about.

I am always excited to learn and improve. Part of my reason for writing this book was because I wanted to learn from others how I could become a better school leader and professional. It is important not to become complacent; even when we are good at something, there is still more to learn. When I thought I had started to improve my public speaking, and was getting used to receiving positive responses, I did an event for a different kind of audience and bombed. One attendee criticised a "lack of robustness with little connected to anything such as reading and wider research". All opinions are subjective but I decided to review my performance, seek feedback and improve and be aware of which audiences I most connected with. As Ryan Holiday says in *Ego is the Enemy,* "The pretense of knowledge is our most dangerous vice because it prevents us from getting any better. Studious self-assessment is the antidote."[5] Each of the leaders I interviewed was clear that their learning never stops. Each of them seemed to have an innate sense of curiosity, which also made them incredibly fun to interview.

---

5 Ryan Holiday, *Ego Is the Enemy: The Fight to Master Our Greatest Opponent* (London: Profile Books, 2017), p. 27.

✳ Not everyone will get you and that's fine

This was quite possibly the most challenging lesson for me. Ben's comments are worth revisiting here: "If your face doesn't fit, do you want to be in an organisation where your face needs to fit?" After speaking to Ben, I had the realisation that there have been one or two times in my career when I realised fairly soon after being hired that I was not a good fit for the organisation and vice versa. Rather than cutting my losses quickly and moving on, I stayed for much longer than I ought to have done because I wanted to prove that I could make it work and maybe, deep down, I saw quitting as failure. Listening to Lila's story of how she knew she had to leave a school where she was overlooked as leadership material because of her introverted nature also made me realise the error of this approach.

You may outgrow the role you were hired for, circumstances may change or a school might not be clear about what they want when they hire you. Whatever the situation, do your best but recognise when you aren't the right fit any more. Move on and don't look back. It can be easy to stay too long. This is usually because you want to see it through and feel like leaving would mean admitting that you made a mistake or feeling like a failure. It's not a failure. It's a learning process. Reflect. Learn. Move on. Wish the school the best and make a different mistake next time. We're always making mistakes; it's fine as long as they aren't always the same ones.

✳ Be aware of the lines you won't cross

This was a clear part of Scarlet's story and she felt compelled to leave her school as a result, but she wasn't the only person who mentioned having red lines that they would not cross professionally. Each of the leaders I interviewed had a very clear sense of self that had evolved over time. This enabled them to know what they believed and what they would and wouldn't do in their professional lives. You won't agree with everything and everybody at work and most disagreements aren't resigning issues. Part of leadership and maturity is compromise. Be aware of what you will not compromise on and act according to your conscience.

Malcolm told me more about the incident that made him leave his job as a senior manager in IT to become a teacher:

> "I worked in one particular company where I was responsible for a large number of staff, all people who, when I started, were on the worst salaries, really badly treated. I fought to get every single person on the right kind of money but conditional on that, we need to make this department work. We were really successful. But my boss said to me one day, 'You need to get rid of five people, Malcolm. We need a higher margin.' So I went back in and made the amount of money that would have been saved by getting rid of them. But he still wanted me to fire more people. That was my red line. I wasn't prepared to make people needlessly redundant. Within three months I'd left that organisation and was training to be a teacher."

After Malcolm had left, his manager asked him to come back. When you know what your values are and act accordingly, you will respect yourself and so will other people.

✳ Collaborate, even with people who aren't like you

To achieve anything meaningful you need to be able to work with a variety of people. Some will agree with you, others won't. Either way, it's not the end of the world. Many of the leaders I spoke to mentioned how important it is to build a network of like-minded peers. However, it's just as important to be able to collaborate with people who aren't like you. Lila, for example, mentioned how she interviewed two equally competent candidates for a deputy headship position, but ultimately chose the one who was least like her in order to add different strengths to her team. Malcolm was explicit about the need to understand the politics of a school, while Tait was clear that he didn't expect everyone to agree with him, and welcomed a diversity of opinion, as long as people were thinking about the issues. Leah reflected that her period as acting head teacher was made easier because she was co-leading with someone:

"I was incredibly lucky that I was going through it with somebody else. We were there for each other. We weren't actually that close before that but now I think we get on a lot better. It was a kind of bonding experience."

✳ The people you look up to have struggled too

It's easy to look at people you respect and admire and think that they have it all together, that they have always been as good as you perceive them to be now. This isn't true. Many of the leaders I spoke to told me of times in their careers when they weren't as skilled as people regard them now. Tait, a respected senior leader and author, told me about when he was a young teacher and a student got on the floor and started barking like a dog during his lesson. The class descended into anarchy and he felt powerless as he struggled to regain control. It reminded me of the time when a child in my class randomly started chanting "ruler, ruler" in a possessed, weird horror film type voice while I was trying to teach a maths lesson (at least it was a subject-relevant chant). We've all had moments when we've been derailed and felt like we don't know what to do. Any honest and reflective leader will be clear that learning from failure and continually improving and developing their expertise has been key to their success.

Aside from failures related to technical skills as a teacher or leader, the theme of personal struggle – sometimes profoundly affecting mental health – also runs throughout many of these leaders' stories. I am adamant that my own breakdown, although horrible and life-sapping at the time, was one of the best things to have happened to me professionally and personally. Considering my own experience in retrospect and digesting the stories of disappointment, pain and subsequent growth that leaders like Allana, Scarlet and Leah have shared has made me confidently agree with the author and advocate of stoicism Ryan Holiday when he writes, "there is always some good – even if only barely perceptible at first – contained within the bad."[6]

---

6 Ryan Holiday, *The Obstacle Is the Way: The Ancient Art of Turning Adversity to Advantage* (London: Profile Books, 2015), p. 155.

✳ A break from school can enhance your leadership

Your career does not need to go in a straight line or climb the traditional ladder. In *Lean In*, Sheryl Sandberg, chief operating officer of Facebook, writes of a career jungle gym where you can choose different paths that lead to the same destination.[7] Scarlet compared leadership to a slinky, not always following a straight path. Tait, Scarlet, Lila and Karen all explicitly mentioned taking significant breaks from the traditional school environment. Tait described his year as a borough adviser as his own "sabbatical", in which he was able to learn from a variety of school environments and do a lot of thinking and reading that would ultimately shape his approach to teaching, learning and school leadership when he returned to the classroom.

✳ Self-awareness is your strength

Each of the leaders had a very clear personal story about why they became a teacher, some straight out of university, others as career changers. Some were driven to work in schools serving a particular type of community. Others were shaped by their own formative experiences and the value that their parents placed on education. Others didn't want to see the disadvantages that they'd experienced perpetuated. Lila has an intimate personal connection with the community that her school serves because many of the students are from families who fled East Africa at the same time hers did in the 1970s. Malcolm has chosen to work in schools where he feels able to tackle what he calls "intersections of disadvantage", whether this is in a city or rural environment.

I once spoke to the head teacher of an inner-city London school, who was fairly early into his first headship. He told me that prior to that role, he kept getting invited to interview but was always rejected. He couldn't work out why; he was as experienced and well-qualified as the other candidates, he thought. When he spoke to somebody in his network, they told him it wasn't clear why he

---

7   Sheryl Sandberg, *Lean In: Women, Work, and the Will to Lead* (London: WH Allen, 2013).

specifically wanted to lead in the types of schools he was applying for. What did he believe about education? What experiences had shaped him and his beliefs? He reflected on these words – and on his life and career to date – and worked out what he believed, why and, crucially, how to articulate it. Then he got the next headship position he applied for. I was impressed by his vision and it was certainly clear when you spoke to him and visited his school. So clear and impressive, in fact, I applied for a job as one of his deputies – which is how we met.[8]

Parting words

I started writing this book as an assistant head teacher who was often assumed to be on the path to headship. While writing, I decided that I no longer wanted to be a school leader and returned to classroom teaching part-time as I planned to make the transition out of the profession. That process took two years and it flew by because I realised that there was much I still loved about teaching teenagers. As I write this conclusion, over two years after interviewing the first school leader, I realise what a journey the book and I have been on. It has morphed from being about how I could find a way to survive and thrive as a school leader, as somebody who routinely felt that they didn't fit the mould, to being a guide for others who still work in the system.

A few days before writing this I was about to disappear to the local coffee shop to do some final editing. My son was sitting at the kitchen table as I packed my rucksack and asked what I was doing. I told him I was finishing off my book and he asked what it was about. It was then that I realised that, although he and his sisters knew I was writing one, I hadn't really explained what it was about because I didn't think they would find it interesting. Here, I thought, was a chance to explain it in terms that a 7-year-old could understand, and I had to make it sound interesting, so I did my best. Then my partner came in and asked what we'd been talking about. My son told her we'd been discussing my book:

---

8   I didn't get the job, for those of you interested. It was during the period of knowing that I needed a change but not being sure what it was, as outlined in the preface.

"It's for people like Mrs Ginger to help them be better at their jobs but also to be proud of who they are."[9]

I encourage you to embrace being an unexpected leader. Do not worry about fitting the mould. Break the mould. Create your own. Keep learning and do the best for the young people and staff you are responsible for, but, above all, look after yourself while you are doing it. Finally, hold the door open for others, share knowledge and help other unexpected leaders to develop and thrive too.

9 Mrs Ginger is the deputy head of our kids' primary school.

Bibliography

Abrams, Fran (2012). Is the New Chief Inspector of Schools Just an Instrument of Government?, *The Guardian* (23 January). Available at: https://www.theguardian.com/education/2012/jan/23/chief-inspector-schools-michael-wilshaw.

Aliakbari, Mohammad and Elham Faraji (2011). Basic Principles of Critical Pedagogy, *International Proceedings of Economics Development and Research* 17: 77–85. Available at: http://www.ipedr.com/vol17/14-CHHSS%202011-H00057.pdf.

Anonymous (2017). 'Sacked from the School I Loved': A Headteacher's Story, *The Guardian* (24 October). Available at: https://www.theguardian.com/education/2017/oct/24/sacked-school-headteacher-alevel-results.

Bonetti, Sarah (2018). *The Early Years Workforce: A Fragmented Picture* (London: Education Policy Institute). Available at: https://epi.org.uk/publications-and-research/early-years-workforce_analysis/.

Broadcasters (2018). Michaela Coel: MacTaggart Lecture in Full, *Broadcast Now* (23 August). Available at: https://www.broadcastnow.co.uk/broadcasters/michaela-coel-mactaggart-lecture-in-full/5131910.article.

Bulman, May (2017). Primary School Teachers' Suicide Rate Nearly Double National Average, Figures Reveal, *The Independent* (17 March). Available at: https://www.independent.co.uk/news/uk/home-news/primary-school-teachers-suicide-rate-double-national-average-uk-figures-a7635846.html.

Busby, Eleanor (2018). Three in 10 New School Leaders Quit in the First Five Years, Figures Reveal, *The Independent* (5 May). Available at: https://www.independent.co.uk/news/education/education-news/school-leaders-headteachers-quit-teacher-retention-crisis-angela-rayner-labour-naht-a8337661.html.

Cain, Susan (2013). *Quiet: The Power of Introverts in a World That Can't Stop Talking* (London: Penguin).

Carlile, Alex (2011). *Report to the Home Secretary of Independent Oversight of Prevent Review and Strategy* (London: Home Office). Available at: https://assets.publishing.service.gov.uk/government/uploads/system/uploads/attachment_data/file/97977/lord-carlile-report.pdf.

Coles, Tait (2014). Critical Pedagogy: Schools Must Equip Students to Challenge the Status Quo, *The Guardian* (25 February). Available at: https://www.theguardian.com/teacher-network/teacher-blog/2014/feb/25/critical-pedagogy-schools-students-challenge.

Coles, Tait (2014). *Never Mind the Inspectors: Here's Punk Learning* (Carmarthen: Independent Thinking Press).

Cordingley, Philippa and Miranda Bell (2012). *Understanding What Enables High Quality Professional Learning: A Report on the Research Evidence* (CUREE and Pearson School Improvement). Available at: http://www.curee.co.uk/publication/understanding-what-enables-high-quality-professional-learning.

Covey, Stephen R. (1989). *The Seven Habits of Highly Successful People: Powerful Lessons in Personal Change* (London: Simon & Schuster).

Dabell, John (2017). Punk Learning, *Teacher Toolkit* [blog] (12 March). Available at: https://www.teachertoolkit.co.uk/2017/03/12/punk-learning/.

Department for Education (2018). Reducing Teacher Workload: Policy Paper (24 July). Available at: https://www.gov.uk/government/publications/reducing-teachers-workload/reducing-teachers-workload.

Department for Education (2018). Regional, LA and School Tables: School Workforce Census 2017 (28 June). Available at: https://www.gov.uk/government/statistics/school-workforce-in-england-november-2017.

Department for Education (2018). Revised GCSE and Equivalent Results in England: 2016 to 2017. Ref: SFR01/2018 [statistical first release] (25 January). Available at: https://www.gov.uk/government/statistics/revised-gcse-and-equivalent-results-in-england-2016-to-2017.

Department for Education (2018). School Workforce in England: November 2017. Tables: School Workforce Census 2017 (28 June). Available at: https://www.gov.uk/government/statistics/school-workforce-in-england-november-2017.

Featherstone, Keziah (2018). Punk Leadership Means Daring to Think Outside the System, *Schools Week* (23 June). Available at: https://schoolsweek.co.uk/punk-leadership-means-daring-to-think-outside-the-system/.

Ferriss, Tim (2016). *Tools of Titans: The Tactics, Routines, and Habits of Billionaires, Icons, and World-Class Performers* (London: Vermilion).

Fey, Tina (2011). *Bossypants* (London: Sphere).

Goins, Jeff (2017). *Real Artists Don't Starve: Timeless Strategies for Thriving in the New Creative Age* (Nashville, TN: Nelson Books).

Haque, Zubaida and Sian Elliott (2016). *Visible and Invisible Barriers: The Impact of Racism on BME Teachers* (London: Runnymede Trust and National Union of Teachers). Available at: https://www.teachers.org.uk/sites/default/files2014/barriers-report.pdf.

Hazell, Will (2017). Teachers Work a 54-Hour Week, DfE Survey Finds, *TES* (24 February). Available at: https://www.tes.com/news/teachers-work-54-hour-week-dfe-survey-finds.

Higton, John, Sarah Leonardi, Neil Richards, Arifa Choudhoury, Nicholas Sofroniou and David Owen (2017). *Teacher Workload Survey 2016: Research Report* (London: Department for Education). Available at: https://assets.publishing.service.gov.uk/government/uploads/system/uploads/attachment_data/file/592499/TWS_2016_FINAL_Research_report_Feb_2017.pdf.

Hoffman, Reid (n.d.). Infinite Learner, *Masters of Scale*, episode 14 [podcast]. Available at: https://mastersofscale.com/barry-diller-infinite-learner-2/.

Holiday, Ryan (2015). *The Obstacle Is the Way: The Ancient Art of Turning Adversity to Advantage* (London: Profile Books).

Holiday, Ryan (2017). *Ego Is the Enemy: The Fight to Master Our Greatest Opponent* (London: Profile Books).

Home Office (2011). *Prevent Review: Summary of Responses to the Consultation* (June). Available at: https://assets.publishing.service.gov.uk/government/uploads/system/uploads/attachment_data/file/97978/prevent-summary-consultation.pdf.

Home Office and the Rt Hon Theresa May MP (2011). New Prevent Strategy Launched [press release] (7 June). Available at: https://www.gov.uk/government/news/new-prevent-strategy-launched.

Kleon, Austin (2014). *Show Your Work! 10 Things Nobody Told You About Getting Discovered* (New York: Workman Publishing).

LB Hackney Policy Team (2018). *A Profile of Hackney, its People and Place*, Document Number: 18909115 (January). Available at: https://www.hackney.gov.uk/population?.

Menzies, Loic, Meenakshi Parameshwaran, Anna Trethewey, Bart Shaw, Sam Baars and Charleen Chiong (2015). *Why Teach?* (LKMco and Pearson). Available at: http://whyteach.lkmco.org/wp-content/uploads/2015/10/Embargoed-until-Friday-23-October-2015-Why-Teach.pdf.

Myatt, Mary (2016). *High Challenge, Low Threat: How the Best Leaders Find the Balance* (Woodbridge: John Catt Educational).

National Day Nurseries Association (2018). *NDNA 2017/18 Workforce Survey.* Available at: https://www.ndna.org.uk/NDNA/News/Reports_and_surveys/Workforce_survey/Workforce_survey_2018.aspx.

Pells, Rachael (2017). Black and Ethnic Minority Teachers Face 'Invisible Glass Ceiling' in Schools, Report Warns, *The Independent* (14 April). Available at: https://www.independent.co.uk/news/education/education-news/black-asian-ethnic-minority-teachers-invisible-glass-ceiling-racism-schools-report-runnymeade-nut-a7682026.html.

Pells, Rachael (2017). One in Ten Teachers Taking Antidepressants to Cope with Work Stresses, *The Independent* (16 April). Available at: https://www.independent.co.uk/news/education/education-news/teachers-antidepressants-stress-workload-suicidal-one-in-ten-nasuwt-a7684466.html.

Perera, Natalie, Jon Andrews and Peter Sellen (2017). *The Implications of the National Funding Formula for Schools* (London: Education Policy Institute). Available at: https://epi.org.uk/publications-and-research/implications-national-funding-formula-schools/.

Roberts, John (2018). Is Ofsted Fit to Judge Deprived Schools?, *TES* (16 June) Available at: https://www.tes.com/news/ofsted-fit-judge-deprived-schools.

Sandberg, Sheryl (2013). *Lean In: Women, Work, and the Will to Lead* (London: WH Allen).

Secret Teacher, The (2016). Secret Teacher: I Protect and Nurture My Staff Like a Doting Parent, *The Guardian* (4 June). Available at: https://www.theguardian.com/teacher-network/2016/jun/04/secret-teacher-protect-nurture-staff-parent-senior-leadership-team.

Shaw, Bart, Loic Menzies, Eleanor Bernardes, Sam Baars, Philip Nye and Rebecca Allen (2016). *Ethnicity, Gender and Social Mobility* (London: Social Mobility Commission). Available at: https://assets.publishing.service.gov.uk/government/uploads/system/uploads/attachment_data/file/579988/Ethnicity_gender_and_social_mobility.pdf.

Shukla, Nikesh (ed.) (2016). *The Good Immigrant* (London: Unbound).

Smith, Patti (2010). *Just Kids* (London: Bloomsbury).

Sobel, Andrew and Jerold Panas (2012). *Power Questions: Build Relationships, Win New Business, and Influence Others* (Hoboken, NJ: John Wiley and Sons).

TUC (2017). Workers in the UK Put in £33.6 Billion Worth of Unpaid Overtime a Year, Trades Union Congress [press release] (24 February). Available at: https://www.tuc.org.uk/news/workers-uk-put-%C2%A3336-billion-worth-unpaid-overtime-year.

Williamson, Cheryl (2017). Servant Leadership: How to Put Your People Before Yourself, *Forbes* (19 July). Available at: https://www.forbes.com/sites/forbescoachescouncil/2017/07/19/servant-leadership-how-to-put-your-people-before-yourself/#55e6b85066bc.

Worth, Jack, Susan Bamford and Ben Durbin (2015). *Should I Stay or Should I Go? NFER Analysis of Teachers Joining and Leaving the Profession* (Slough: NFER). Available at: https://www.nfer.ac.uk/publications/LFSA01/LFSA01.pdf.

Worth, Jack (2018). The UK's Teacher Supply Is Leaking … and Fast, *TES* [blog] (28 June). Available at: https://www.tes.com/news/uks-teacher-supply-leaking-and-fast.

Resources

This is not a how-to book but I wanted to include some further resources which offer additional practical tips related to some of the chapters:

Iesha Small, 3 Steps I Took to Narrowly Avoid Burnout, *Iesha Small* [blog] (4 March 2018). Available at: https://ieshasmall.com/3-steps-i-took-to-narrowly-avoid-burnout/.

This post is the first I wrote explicitly about burnout and overwhelm on my professional blog. I was trying to finish this book while working two jobs and had taken on too many other commitments. I received a massive response to this post, with a number of teachers and other professionals saying that they also felt like this and telling me how they had used the practical suggestions given to feel in control again.

Iesha Small, 5 Simple Habits That Will Transform Your Mental Health, *Iesha Small* [blog] (25 March 2018). Available at: https://ieshasmall.com/5-simple-daily-habits-that-will-transform-your-mental-health/.

If the previous blog post is about avoiding falling into the abyss, then this one is about the daily maintenance that will keep you mentally healthy and ensure your work doesn't consume you. It outlines the practices that I have been using for a few years to help me manage my depression without medication. Again, I must stress that this is just advice that has worked for me. Please seek appropriate medical help if needed.

Iesha Small, How to Bounce Back from Negative Feedback or Criticism That Wounds You, *Iesha Small* [blog] (10 June 2018). Available at: https://ieshasmall.com/how-to-bounce-back-when-you-receive-negative-feedback-or-criticism-that-wounds-you-insid/.

Resilience is a real feature of being an unexpected Leader. Occasionally we all receive negative feedback that, for whatever reason, affects us particularly badly; this blog outlines how to deal with it and how to work out which negative feedback you can learn from and which is more about the person giving it and needs to be discounted.

Iesha Small, #24 Eleanor Bernardes: Networking and Professional Relationships, *lkmco* [podcast] (16 July 2018). Available at: https://www.lkmco.org/podcast/024-eleanor-bernardes-networking-and-professional-relationships/.
Building professional networks is a theme throughout *The Unexpected Leader*. In this podcast, I interview Eleanor about how to build long-lasting networks and professional relationships in a way that feels natural to you and isn't gross.

Kelly Long, Episode 51: Iesha Small, Part 1: Unconventional Leadership, *Inspiration 4 Teachers* [podcast] (10 January 2016). Available at: https://itunes.apple.com/gb/podcast/51-iesha-small-part-1-educational-leadership-series/id955333603?i=1000360414172&mt=2.

In this podcast, I'm interviewed about my views and philosophy relating to education and school leadership. I was still an assistant head when I recorded this and had a number of staff at my school come and talk to me about my ideas afterwards.

Iesha Small Newsletter. Available at: https://ieshasmall.com/newsletter/.

Subscribe to my newsletter for ongoing tips and ideas. I write regularly about education and leadership and I also sporadically share interesting things that I come across. My main aim is to support you to lead effectively, bring your whole self to work and have the tools to be mentally resilient in your leadership and wider life. You'll also get a free copy of my '9 lessons for unexpected leaders' pdf.

Unexpected Leader Bonus Materials. Available at: https://ieshasmall.com/unexpectedleaderbonus.

An additional chapter on a hidden page especially for my readers.

I hope that we can join one another to continue the conversation about how to break the mould for school leadership and other sectors of society that make a real difference to people's lives, while enabling others to do the same.

Find me on Twitter @ieshasmall.

About the author

Iesha Small is an educator, a writer and a senior associate at an education think tank.

Iesha was previously an assistant head teacher and taught maths for fourteen years in schools in London and the east of England. After a breakdown in 2011, Iesha started using photography to improve her mental health and explore other people's stories via her multimedia project Mindshackles.[1] Iesha is a monthly columnist for *Schools Week* and has written for other major education media outlets such as *TES* and the *Teacher Toolkit* blog. To keep things interesting, she is also a speaker, blogger and podcaster. *The Unexpected Leader* is Iesha's first book. She lives near London with her family and a tiny but loud dog.

Iesha can be found online at ieshasmall.com.

---

1 See https://www.mindshackles.co.uk/.